TWO VIEWS OF THE CROSS
ORTHODOXY AND THE WEST

FREDERICA MATHEWES-GREEN

Felicity Press

First Printing 2022

Two Views of the Cross: Orthodoxy and the West

Copyright © 2022 by Frederica Mathewes-Green

Paperback ISBN: 978-1-0881-0025-7

Portions of this book previously appeared in:

Welcome to the Orthodox Church by

Frederica Mathewes-Green

Copyright © 2015 by Frederica Mathewes-Green

Used by permission of Paraclete Press, www.paracletepress.com

Cover art:

Left: *Icon of the Crucifixion,* Greek processional icon, 14th c.

Photographer: George E. Koronaios

Source: Wikimedia Commons

License: Creative Commons Attribution-Share Alike 4.0.

Right: *The Crucifixion with the Virgin and St. John*

Artist: Hendrick ter Brugghen, 1624-5

Source: Wikimedia Commons

License: Public Domain

All rights reserved. No portion of this book may be reproduced, stored in an electronic retrieval system, or transmitted in any form or by any means—electronic, mechanical, photocopy, recording, or any other—except for brief quotations in printed reviews, without the prior permission of the publisher.

Published by Felicity Press

Johnson City, TN

www.Frederica.com

 Created with Vellum

*In memory of
my beloved spiritual father,
Fr. George Calciu,
who defeated evil
by suffering*

ALSO BY FREDERICA MATHEWES-GREEN

- Welcome to the Orthodox Church: An Introduction to Eastern Christianity *(Paraclete Press, 2015)*
- The Jesus Prayer: The Ancient Desert Prayer that Tunes the Heart to God *(Paraclete Press, 2009)*
- Mary as the Early Christians Knew Her: The Mother of Jesus in Three Ancient Texts *(Paraclete Press, 2007)*
- First Fruits of Prayer: A Forty-Day Journey through the Canon of St. Andrew *(Paraclete Press, 2005)*
- The Open Door: Entering the Sanctuary of Icons and Prayer *(Paraclete Press, 2003)*
- Gender: Men, Women, Sex, Feminism *(Ancient Faith Publishing, 2002)*
- The Illumined Heart: The Ancient Christian Path of Transformation *(Paraclete Press, 2001)*
- At the Corner of East and Now: A Modern Life in Ancient Christian Orthodoxy *(Ancient Faith Press, 2009; Tarcher/Penguin Putnam, 1999)*

- Facing East: A Pilgrim's Journey into the Mysteries of Orthodoxy *(HarperSanFrancisco, 1997)*

- Real Choices: Listening to Women, Looking for Alternatives to Abortion *(Felicity Press, 2014; Conciliar Press, 1997; Multnomah Press, 1994)*

Audiobooks available for most titles

A NOTE ON TERMINOLOGY

The general topic of Christ's sacrifice on the Cross, and how it enabled our salvation, is usually called "the atonement." The term was coined by English-speakers a few centuries ago, and signifies "at-one-ment." Though the word is not familiar to the historic lands and languages of Orthodoxy, the concept of at-one-ment with God is one that Orthodox Christians would warmly embrace.

1
THREE DIRECTIONS OF BIBLICAL LANGUAGE

C hrist's death on the Cross is our salvation; on this, Christians East and West agree. But how does that work, exactly?

As a Protestant (before I became Orthodox, decades ago), I had a clear understanding of the means of our salvation. Because of our sins, we humans owe an immense debt to God. It is greater than we could ever repay. Christ took on human form and died on the Cross, as a sacrifice to the Father. He paid the debt for us, and now we can receive salvation as a free gift. By accepting Christ's work on our behalf, we are delivered from eternal punishment in Hell, and can receive eternal life in Heaven.

I thought the only alternative to that view was to think that we humans are obliged to add some "good works" to the balance, as our own contribution toward the debt. I scoffed at that idea. But both views had the same premise: God could not forgive us until the sin-debt was paid.

But Orthodox Christians don't see the Cross as a

payment to God for our sins. They think of it primarily as a *victory*—a triumph over death and the evil one.

The Orthodox account of salvation begins the same way as that of other Christians: we all are sinners (Romans 3:23), and death is the price of sin (Romans 6:23). Before the coming of Christ, all of humanity, even the righteous, departed this life to be bound and imprisoned in Hades.

Christ put on our human nature so he could die and enter Hades, appearing to be just one more captive human. But once he entered the devil's lair, he revealed his divinity and power. He broke down the gates of Hades and bound the devil in his own chains. He lifted Adam and Eve from their tombs, freeing all the righteous dead from their captivity.

When Western Christians hear this description they're apt to say, "We believe that, too!" There's naturally a fair amount of overlap, since we're all reading the same New Testament.

So let's lay out the strands distinctly. Biblical language about salvation points in at least three directions:

- We have been delivered from Death; the evil one is defeated and his captives are set free. This is powerfully foreshadowed by the deliverance of the Hebrew people at the Red Sea. Terms referring to this aspect of salvation include **Ransomed, Redeemed, Delivered,** and **Saved**.

- We have been restored to a right relationship with God. The parable of the Prodigal Son beautifully illustrates the Father's love and acceptance of us, even "while we were yet sinners" (Romans 5:8). This aspect of salvation is expressed in words like **Forgiveness** and **Mercy**.

- The Father accepts his Son's self-offering, as the "new covenant in [his] blood" (Luke 22:20). The entirety of the Hebrew system of sacrifices was a foreshadowing of the Cross. Now we find terms like **Sacrifice** and **Offering.**

In the upcoming chapters, we'll take a closer look at those Scriptures, and explore the Orthodox understanding of salvation. It all begins with the victory of the Cross.

2

BUT MY THEOLOGY IS BASED ON THE BIBLE!

We'd better get out of the way now. As a Protestant, I would have protested that *my* theological perspective was clearly better than anyone else's. *Mine* was based on the Bible.

But the Orthodox Church's theology is based on the Bible, too. Actually, *all* churches can say their theology is based on the Bible—and prove it, too. They just interpret it differently.

We Orthodox hold an ace card, though. We *wrote* the Bible.

Well, the New Testament, anyway. St. Paul, St. Matthew, and the rest were born in the Middle East. People of those lands were the first to follow Christ, and then the first to "go into all the world to preach the Gospel" (Mark 16:15). They wrote the New Testament in *koine* Greek, the common language of trade. Despite centuries of horrific persecution and invasion, the indigenous Christian faith in the Bible lands is still Orthodox.

And it is a *united* faith. That's one of the big surprises

about Orthodoxy, that its theology stays the same, century after century, from one land and culture to the next. Western Christianity hasn't enjoyed such continuity; in any American city you'll find wildly different varieties of Christian faith, even within the same denomination. In a bitter irony, sincere love of Scripture led to entrenched and endless quarreling.

There was another problem. Western Christian theology was founded solidly on the Scriptures—as read *in Latin translation*.[1] In the 1100 years between St. Jerome's Latin translation of the Bible (the *Vulgate*, AD 405) and the onset of the Reformation (1517), some of what the Greek conveys had been lost.

For example, Latin didn't have an equivalent for the Greek word *energeia* (energy), so Jerome used the Latin *operatio* (operation). But word choice can subtly shift a meaning. In Philippians 2:13, is God "operating" in you like a puppeteer, or "energizing" within you, filling you with his presence, grace, and power?

When Western Christians discuss theology today, they usually cite theological authorities of the last few centuries. But Orthodox Christians can call on the writers of the early church, who were and still are members of their larger congregation. Middle-eastern, Greek-speaking Christians wrote the New Testament, and were its target audience, too. We don't have to claim that they were holier or wiser than other Christians to recognize that this gives them an edge, when it comes to interpreting the Bible.

So that's the ace. Over the centuries and around the globe, Orthodox Christians have perpetuated that faith unchanged; it is remarkable, indeed miraculous, how consistently it appears, even among countries with no contact with each other, even among those at enmity with each other. That pervasive early understanding of the Scriptures, passed on intact from one generation to the next, within each "tribe and tongue and people and nation" (Revelation 5:9), without any pope or world-wide leader—that united and ancient faith is the foundation of the Orthodox understanding of salvation, right from the start.

3
RANSOMED, REDEEMED, DELIVERED, AND SAVED

Let's start with the first of those three sets of biblical terms, **Ransomed, Redeemed, Delivered,** and **Saved.** This was the part that surprised me the most. As I came to understand the Orthodox view of salvation, I had to reorganize a lot of my mental furniture.

As a Protestant, I associated those ransom-redeem terms with Christ dying on the Cross, an offering to God in full payment for our sins. But, if you think about it, Christ's offering to the Father doesn't belong in the **Ransom-Redeem** category; it comes up later, in the **Sacrifices** and **Offerings** department. For now, we're looking only at words that have the sense of "rescue."

In koine Greek, the word we translate "salvation" is *soteria*. Christ is "the *soter* of the *kosmos*," the Savior of the world (John 4:42). This is salvation in the sense of being rescued from evil, attack, and danger. It's "saved" as in "saved from drowning."

We didn't need to be rescued from the *Father*. We needed to be rescued from *Death*.

I'll give that a capital letter, for in Orthodox theology Death is not merely the end of earthly life, but an active, destructive force, closely allied with the evil one.

As a Western Christian I had the vague idea that some people believe in "the harrowing of Hell," but the concept didn't take up much room in my understanding of salvation. For Orthodox, though, it's the great turning-point of the story. Everything takes its place around this central truth: Death has been slain; Christ's victory in Hades delivers us from Death. [1]

Ever since the Fall of Adam and Eve ("the Ancestral Sin," as Orthodox call it), every person has been born with a fatal susceptibility to sin. ("All have sinned and fall short of the glory of God," Romans 3:23.) Sin poisons us, and makes us captives of the evil one who hates mankind.

For countless millennia, all of humanity, even the righteous of the Old Testament, passed through the gates of Death and took up residence in the realm of Hades. ("The wages of sin is death," Romans 6:23.) All were excluded from Paradise, the home God had prepared for us from the beginning.

Though we disobeyed, God loved us. He had a just claim upon us: he made us in his "image [and] likeness" (Genesis 1:26), so we belong to him by right. He would not allow his people to remain captives of the evil one.

Christ came to our rescue. When he was conceived in Mary's womb, he began the healing of our common human nature, by infusing it with his own eternal life. He then followed our common path into Death ("While we were yet sinners, Christ died for us," Romans 5:23), but once there he destroyed its power, setting us free. Christ poured his Life into the realm of Death, like light pouring into a darkened room.

The icon of the Resurrection depicts this victory. A particularly compelling example is a 14th c. ceiling fresco in the Church of Chora, near Istanbul. Christ is centered in the image, robed in radiant white, standing on the broken gates of Hades. He is braced and striding, pulling Adam and Eve from their stony tombs, and they come up flying; he grasps them by their wrists, not their hands, for all power streams from him.

On one side, King David, King Solomon, and St. John the Baptist (now re-capitated) marvel at this wondrous sight; on the other, the righteous of all ages wait their turn. Abel, holding his shepherd's staff, stands first in line behind his mother. Below Christ's feet, beneath the fallen gates of Hades, is a dark pit strewn with broken chains and locks; there we see the evil one, bound in his own fetters.

The Scriptures speak of Christ's work in Hades:

"So will the Son of Man be three days and three nights in the heart of the earth" (Matthew 12:40).

"The hour is coming, and now is, when the dead will hear the voice of the Son of God, and those who hear will live" (John 5:25).

"The last enemy to be destroyed is death" (1 Corinthians 15:26).

"Therefore it is said, 'When he ascended on high he led a host of captives, and he gave gifts to men' [Psalm 67/68:18][2]. In saying, 'He ascended,' what does it mean but that he had also descended into the lower parts of the earth? He who descended is he who also ascended far above all the heavens, that he might fill all things" (Ephesians 4:8-10).

"He disarmed the principalities and powers and made a public example of them, triumphing over them" (Colossians 2:15).

"Since therefore the children share in flesh and blood, he himself likewise partook of the same nature, that through death he might destroy him who has the power of death, that is, the devil, and deliver all those who, through fear of death, were subject to lifelong bondage" (Hebrews 2:14-15).

"[Christ was] put to death in the flesh but made alive in the spirit; in which he went and preached to the spirits in prison, who formerly did not obey" (1 Peter 3:18–20).

"The gospel was preached even to the dead, that though judged in the flesh like men, they might live in the spirit like God" (1 Peter 4:6).

Christian leaders of the first and second century likewise declared Christ's victory over Hades, and his deliverance of the righteous departed:

> Even the prophets, being his disciples, were expecting him as their teacher through the Spirit. And for this cause, he whom they rightly awaited, when he came, raised them from the dead[3] ... He descended, indeed, into Hades alone, but he arose accompanied by a multitude; and rent asunder that means of separation which had existed from

the beginning of the world, and cast down its partition-wall.[4]
   - Ignatius of Antioch (AD 35-108)

Our Lord Jesus Christ, who for our sins suffered even unto death, whom God raised from the dead, having loosed the pangs of Hades.[5]
   - Polycarp (AD 69-155)

The Lord God remembered the people of Israel who lay in the graves, and he descended to preach to them his own salvation.[6]
   - Justin the Martyr (AD 100-165)

For three days he dwelt in the place where the dead were... The Lord remembered his dead saints who slept formerly in the land of burial, and he descended to them, to rescue and save them.[7]
   - Irenaeus (AD 130-202)

    But as a Protestant I sometimes wondered: How had the early Christians known that Christ's Resurrection meant that we would be resurrected too? Why wouldn't they think of it as something that happened to Jesus alone, like the Ascension or the Virgin Birth? (I didn't doubt that we *would* be resurrected; I just wondered how the early Christians arrived at that conclusion.)

    They found it in the Scriptures, of course:

"Lord, you have brought up my soul from Sheol [Hades], restored me to life from among those gone down to the Pit" (Psalm 29/30:3).

"From the depths of the earth you will bring me up again" (Psalm 70/71:20).

"God will ransom my soul from the power of Sheol" (Psalm 48/49:15).

"He will swallow up death for ever, and the Lord God will wipe away tears from all faces" (Isaiah 25:8).

"Because of the blood of my covenant with you, I will set your captives free from the waterless pit" (Zechariah 9:11).

"I will deliver them from the hand of Hades, and I will redeem them from death. O Death, where is your penalty? O Hades, where is your sting?" (Hosea 13:14, 1 Corinthians 15:55)

The early Christians saw Christ's victory in Hades as the center-point of the Gospel story; it is the moment when we are ransomed, redeemed, delivered, and saved. But in the West, the events of Holy Saturday faded in importance, and this dynamic moment-of-rescue was largely forgotten. I have an idea why that happened, and we'll get to it up ahead.

But first I want to tell you a story I came up with (an imperfect one) to represent this idea of salvation as a rescue.

Imagine that some foolish teens dared each other to go to the shady side of town and see if they can buy drugs. But when the drug-dealer sees the kids, he notes their expensive clothing and jewelry and gets bigger ideas. Luring them to an empty apartment, he locks them in and sends a ransom note.

The terrified parents go to the police, and the police chief assembles his officers. He tells them he needs a volunteer for a dangerous mission. He needs someone to go to the kidnapper's lair and break down the door, then let the kids run free. The chief warns, though, that the rescuer himself might be captured and subjected to a miserable death.

A brave officer volunteers, and succeeds in this dangerous mission, delivering the captives to freedom. But, just as had been foretold, he himself is captured. The evil ones seize him, and torture and kill him. (This is where my story breaks down, because I can't say, "But then he comes back to life.")

How should we describe this brave officer's victory? Those foolish teens put themselves in a deadly situation by their own disobedience. They were helpless in the kidnappers' hands; nothing they could do would set them free. It was the brave officer's sacrifice alone that saved them.

He **ransomed** those sinful teens with his blood.
He **redeemed** them at the cost of his life.
He **delivered** them to safety.
He **saved** them from the powers of Death.

Christ **Ransomed, Redeemed, Delivered,** and **Saved** us from the power of Death. As long as we cling to him, repenting of our sins and resisting them as best we can, we are saved. "Whoever calls upon the name of the Lord will be saved" (Romans 10:13).

Pascha (Easter) is by far the most important Feast in the Orthodox Church. The service starts before midnight and runs about three hours, and it's noisy and festive. The priest repeatedly marches through the congregation, swinging a blazing censer and crying out "Christ is risen!," right over the singing of the choir. We shout "Indeed he is risen!" in return, exhausted, hungry (we've been fasting since the afternoon), and yet smiling so much our faces ache. Worn-out children in pajamas lie sleeping all around. The many different elements combine to produce an atmosphere of festive disarray.[8]

By 3:30 AM the whole crowd will be in the parish hall, celebrating this most joyous of Feasts by eating the foods they missed during the long vegan fast, and sharing a convivial glass. Most will be in bed by dawn, and ready to sleep in because they've already been to Sunday morning worship.

The celebration doesn't stop there. In the following weeks, we will keep shouting "Christ is risen!" "Indeed he is risen!" hundreds of times, in a multitude of languages. We will sing, hundreds of times, this brief hymn:

Christ is risen from the dead,
trampling down death by death,
and upon those in the tombs bestowing life!
(St. John of Damascus, AD 675-749)

Christ trampled down our old enemy, Death, by means of his own death. That belief lies at the heart of Orthodox faith.

The best way to grasp the enthusiasm Orthodox Christians have for our rescue from Death is to read the Paschal Sermon of St. John Chrysostom (AD 349-407), which I'll set on the following pages. This lively sermon is preached on Pascha in all Orthodox churches every year, and in some congregations worshippers join in, loudly echoing some of the lines. We hear this sermon only once a year, and anticipate it with relish.

THE PASCHAL SERMON

(c. AD 400)

If anyone is devout and a lover of God, let him enjoy this beautiful and radiant festival.
If anyone is a grateful servant, let him, rejoicing, enter into the joy of his Lord.
If anyone has wearied himself in fasting,
let him now receive recompense.
If anyone has labored from the first hour,
let him today receive the just reward.
If anyone has come at the third hour,
with thanksgiving let him feast.
If anyone has arrived at the sixth hour,
let him have no misgivings, for he shall suffer no loss.
If anyone has delayed until the ninth hour,
let him draw near without hesitation.
If anyone has arrived even at the eleventh hour,
let him not fear on account of tardiness.
For the Master is gracious,

and receives the last even as the first;
He gives rest to him who comes at the eleventh hour,
just as to him who has labored from the first.
He has mercy upon the last and cares for the first;
to the one he gives, and to the other he is gracious.
He both honors the work and praises the intention.

Enter all of you, therefore, into the joy of our Lord,
and, whether first or last, receive your reward.
O rich and poor, one with another, dance for joy!
O you ascetics and you negligent, celebrate the day!
You who fasted and you who disregarded the fast, Rejoice today!
The table is rich-laden: feast royally, all of you!
The calf is fatted: let no one go forth hungry!

Let all partake of the feast of faith.
Let all receive the riches of goodness.

Let no one lament his poverty,
for the universal kingdom has been revealed.
Let no one mourn his transgressions,
for pardon has dawned from the grave.
Let no one fear death,
for the Savior's death has set us free.

He who was taken by Death has annihilated it!
He descended into Hades and took Hades captive!
He embittered it when it tasted His flesh!
And anticipating this, Isaiah exclaimed:
"Hades was embittered when it encountered you
in the lower regions."

It was embittered, for it was abolished!
It was embittered, for it was mocked!
It was embittered, for it was purged!
It was embittered, for it was despoiled!
It was embittered, for it was bound in chains!
It took a body and came upon God!
It took earth and encountered Heaven!
It took what it saw,
and crumbled before what it had not seen!

O Death, where is your sting?
O Hades, where is your victory?

Christ is risen, and you are overthrown!
Christ is risen, and the demons are fallen!
Christ is risen, and the angels rejoice!
Christ is risen, and life reigns!
Christ is risen, and not one dead remains in the tomb!

For Christ, being raised from the dead,
has become the first-fruits of them that have slept.

To him be glory and might unto ages of ages.
Amen.

4
THE PRICE OF "SATISFACTION"

That **Ransom-Redeem** perspective was the primary way of understanding salvation for the early Christians, as it continues to be for Orthodox Christians today. But a millennium after the New Testament was written, on a distant continent, a new idea appeared. It was that Christ's suffering and death paid the Father the great debt we owe for our sins. From rescue to repayment; it made a world of difference.

St. Anselm, Archbishop of Canterbury (AD 1033–1109), was the first to clearly formulate this line of thought. He said that God cannot forgive our sins without punishment, for that would leave sin uncorrected. If God treated sinful and sinless people alike, it would constitute injustice. Anselm reasoned that it was necessary to give God some restitution (or, to use the old term, "satisfaction") to pay the debt for our great offense against his honor.

That would make sense to the people of his time, because the feudal system laid great emphasis on the preservation of honor. A feudal lord was not free to forgive an insult, not even if the offender admitted his guilt and apologized. Such a lord was obliged to demand the satisfaction of his honor, for the social order to be sustained.

Anselm said that, because God's honor is infinitely greater than that of any earthly ruler, no sacrifice humans could make would restore it. Even our own death would not suffice, because we sinners could only be an impure offering. But when Christ died on the Cross, he offered the Father a perfect, holy sacrifice.

However, Christ did not *need* to render a sacrifice to the Father. He gave the Father a satisfaction that he did not owe. Now the Father is obligated to the Son; he owes him a reward.

"One who freely gives so great a gift to God must not be without reward," Anselm wrote. "If the Son willed to give his reward to others, could the Father justly prohibit it, or refuse to bestow it on them?" [1] If the Son wants to bestow his reward on us, how could the Father stop him?

From this point, a shift takes place in Western theology:

Originally, Christ's work is aimed at Death; he defeats it and sets us free.

Now it is aimed at the Father; now, Christ pays our debt so that we can be forgiven.

Originally, salvation was a victory, like the rescue of the Hebrew people at the Red Sea.

Now it is a transaction, whereby we pay our debt to the Father with the Blood of Christ.

The idea that we needed to be saved from Death, our malevolent enemy, begins to diminish.

The idea that we needed to be saved from a just retribution begins to grow.

As thoughtful, intelligent theologians pondered this over the years, they did not insist that Christ died so the Father would be obliged to forgive us. The Father and the Son are one in the Trinity; the one, triune God enacted the plan of salvation. This plan made it possible for God to forgive our sins, they would say, while preserving the balance of justice.

Still, it was easy to see, in the medieval era, how Christ's sacrifice would be akin to satisfying a feudal lord's honor. It's an idea that was easy to grasp, easy to spread.[2]

Time passed, and Anselm's idea was explored by subsequent theologians. Ideas began to emerge and diverge.

And now we're going to walk through rather a blizzard. Don't worry about remembering all this. What I want you to see is how the unity of Western theology was shattered, as dozens, even hundreds, of different ways of interpreting Scripture burst forth. And it all came from the heads of sincere, intelligent, prayerful, Bible-honoring thinkers.

Anselm's idea was that Christ's death satisfies the requirement for restoring God's honor; it's called the **Satisfaction** theory of the atonement. But later theologians saw in Christ's death his acceptance of the "wages of sin" (Romans 6:23) on our behalf. That means Christ is not just satisfying God's honor, he is also taking upon himself the cumulative debt of sin. (A popular saying is, "He paid a debt he did not owe, because we owed a debt we could not pay.")

In doing this he "substitutes" for us, so this may also be called the **Substitutionary** theory of the atonement.

Still other theologians proposed that Christ not only satisfied God's honor, he not only accepted death in our stead, but he also took the *punishment* we deserved. This is the **Penal Substitutionary** theory of the atonement ("penal" as in "penalty").

You see how things keep moving along. In Anselm's theory, Christ died on the Cross so God would not have to punish us for our sins. These later theologians said the Cross *is* the punishment for our sins.

Then some said that Christ not only accepted death as our fate, he not only bore our punishment, but he also absorbed the raw, unbridled *wrath* of God.

Reformation leader John Calvin (AD 1509-1564) espoused this view, writing, "Nothing had been done, if Christ had endured only corporeal death. In order to interpose between us and God's anger, and satisfy his righteous judgment, it was necessary that he should feel the weight of divine vengeance." So Christ "descended to Hell [to undergo] the death which is inflicted on the wicked by an angry God." 3 4

Could things get more complicated? Why not?

There's a short verse of Scripture, 1 John 2:2, that's long provoked disagreement among those who read the Bible in English. The verse reads, "[Christ] is the *hilasmos* for our sins." What's a hilasmos?

Some say it should be translated "expiation." An expiation makes reparation or pays a debt. Expiation aims to make things fair and square.

But others say it means "propitiation." Propitiation aims to appease the *rage* of an offended God.

What does it say in your Bible? If you look up 1 John 2:2,

you might see either "expiation" or "propitiation," depending on the translator's theological leanings.

Let's look in another direction for help: how did the rabbis use "hilasmos" when they translated the Hebrew Old Testament into koine Greek (the Septuagint)? And how did the evangelists and epistolers of the New Testament use it?

The Jewish scholars who produced the Septuagint used "hilasmos" to mean mercy: "Yet there is hilasmos with you" (Psalm 129/130:4). They chose the cognate *hilasterion* as the term for God's throne upon the cherubim (Exodus 25:17–22). "Hilasmos" doesn't have to mean "expiation" or "propitiation"; it could just mean the place where we meet with God and find mercy.

In the New Testament, we find Christ using a cognate of "hilasmos" to mean "mercy." When he says that the penitent Publican prayed "Have mercy on me," the Greek is not the usual *"eleison* me" (as in *Kyrie eleison*), but *"hilastheti* me" (Luke 18:13). Neither "expiation" or "propitiation" make sense there, and translators render it as "mercy."

(Lying behind this translation controversy in the West, I think, is some confusion in our understanding of the Old Testament Temple sacrifices. We'll come back to that.)

The debate over the meaning of "hilasmos" reminds us that Western theology was carefully, thoughtfully, built up from a foundation of reading the Bible in Latin. In the case of "hilasmos," St. Jerome dispensed with the various Latin "mercy" words, and chose the term *propitiatio*.

"He [Christ] is the *propitiatio* for our sins" (1 John 2:2)

"[God] loved us and sent his Son to be the *propitiatio* for our sins" (John 4:10).

"Christ Jesus, whom God put forward as a *propitiatio* by his blood, to be received by faith" Romans (3:25).

"A merciful and faithful high priest in the service of God, to make *propitiatio* for the sins of the people" (Hebrews 2:17).

As Western Christians read the Bible in Latin, they saw Jerome's word choice, *propitatio,* instead of the Latin "mercy" words like *misericordia* and *clementia*. Did this tilt them toward assuming that the Cross was a propitiation for God's wrath?

Here's a startling thought: why do we read translations at all? Once when a new Bible translation was causing controversy, I got an email from a Jewish man who said he had a question, and hoped it wasn't rude. He asked, If Christians love the Bible as much as they say they do, why are they satisfied to read it in translation? Jewish kids learn Hebrew and Muslim kids learn Arabic, so why don't Christians teach their children koine Greek? It's a good question.

Another topic in atonement thinking had to do with the question of *how* to be saved. That's an urgent question, as Jesus warns us repeatedly that there is a place of "torment" (Luke 16:33) and "eternal fire" (Matthew 18:8, 25:41) where the "worm does not die" (Mark 9:48) and there is "weeping and gnashing of teeth" (Matthew 22:13). Jesus clearly believes that there is a Hell, and he knows it's not empty.

How can someone avoid that fate? Historically, Roman Catholics have believed that one must be a baptized and believing member of the Church, and not die with unconfessed mortal sin (grave sin, like murder) on her soul.

Protestants rejected the Roman Catholic claim that salvation was accessible only through that Church. For Protestants, we are saved by God's grace alone, not by anything we do. Salvation can be gained by prayerfully admitting to God that one is a sinner, claiming Christ's death in payment for those sins, and committing oneself to Christ as savior. That's called "the Sinner's Prayer," and it offers a concise entry point to salvation. Since people are free to say this prayer or not, to accept salvation or reject it, this viewpoint is called **Free Will**.

Others insisted that salvation can't be based on *anything* we do—not even saying a prayer. Every human deserves Hell, since "all have sinned" (Romans 3:23). But God chose some ("the elect"), by his inscrutable decree, to receive his grace. Nothing the elect do *earns* them salvation; it's wholly a matter of God's mysterious will. At the end, the elect will receive God's mercy (**Predestination**).

Others add that God likewise decrees who will *not* be saved ("the reprobate"). Bereft of his grace, the reprobate remain mired in sin and will receive, at the end, not God's mercy, but his justice (**Double Predestination**).

All these variations on Christian theology and many more co-exist in the West, and there's no way to determine who's right. It's all a matter of opinion, of personal interpretation. So the fierce conversation keeps rolling on, like a storm across the sea.

5
MERITS AND OTHER MISCHIEF

We began the previous chapter with St. Anselm, and then leapt over a few centuries to trace some of the Protestant variations. But what happened to provoke such protests?

A central theme of the Protestant Reformation, sweeping Europe in the 1500s, was rejection of the Catholic Church's claim to be the sole source of salvation. As above, Protestants insisted that Christ's death on the Cross paid the entire sin-debt for all time. There is no leftover debt for us humans to pay.

In the Catholic understanding, though, there's a distinction. Christ paid the **eternal** debt for our sins; our guilt is completely absolved (after baptism and sacramental confession). But there remains the **temporal** debt, which we ourselves must pay, either in this life, or in Purgatory after death.[1] Since this is a debt we can eventually pay off, it is temporary—temporal, not eternal.

The Catholic Church claims the authority to grant remission of this temporal debt, by applying the merits of Christ and the saints. The thinking goes like this: Christ's sacrifice was so great that even a single drop of his blood would have sufficed for all the sins of humankind. There are, as well, the sinless Virgin Mary and other saints, who accomplished holy deeds surpassing their own salvific needs. That means there is an abundance of unused, leftover merits.

(Now watch that little word "merit." It's not in the Bible. It's not a biblical concept! "Merit" is like a mouse in the pantry; it never should have gotten into things in the first place.)

These extra merits accumulate in the **Treasury of Merit**, administered by the Roman Catholic Church. Merits can be applied in the form of **indulgences,** to lighten sinners' temporal punishment. These indulgences are gained by performing specific holy deeds or saying particular prayers. The Council of Trent (mid-1500's) condemned anyone who denied the efficacy of indulgences, which places this doctrine among those termed infallible.

The classic Protestant response is that we are saved by the merits of Christ alone; no good deeds on our part, or those of any saint, are necessary. God **imputes** or **imparts** (those are distinct theological terms) Christ's merits to us, so that we appear as righteous in his sight. (There's a counter-argument that, if God sees us as righteous though we are not, it amounts to a legal fiction.)

Other theologians, finding all this too legalistic, proposed that Christ came simply to teach, inspire, and provide us with a good example (the **Moral Influence** theory). In this view, the pathos of Christ's self-sacrificing death draws the Father and humanity into loving reconciliation.

You'll hear something similar today, as people assert that

Christ was not divine, but merely a wise teacher who gave us a good example to follow. St. Augustine responded to an ancient version of this idea by saying that, if imitation of a righteous man were all we needed, we wouldn't speak of "Adam and Christ" but "Adam and Abel." Adam's virtuous son provided a fine example. We needed more than that.[2]

With the advent of the Enlightenment in the 18th century, many intellectuals rejected the idea of revealed religion entirely. They recognized that the universe was obviously created by a God, but said that he doesn't intervene in its affairs (**Deism**). A popular image was that of a watchmaker who creates an intricate and beautiful timepiece, and then walks away, leaving only the evidence of his genius behind.

That "walking away" is part of the soft-headed theory that creeps through much of Western Christianity today. It was named **Moralistic Therapeutic Deism** (**MTD**) by sociologists Christian Smith and Melinda Denton, in their book *Soul Searching*.

MTD comprises these beliefs:

Moralistic—God wants us to be "good" or "nice," in a vague and general sense. Everyone considers herself "good" and feels confident she will go to Heaven.

Therapeutic—We can call on God when we need help or want to feel better.

Deism—Other than that, God is not much involved in human life.

There is no theory of atonement with **MTD**, because no

one thinks he is a sinner. God is like a kindly old man, keeping watch over us. C. S. Lewis wrote, "We want, in fact, not so much a Father in heaven as a grandfather in heaven— a senile benevolence who, as they say, 'liked to see young people enjoying themselves.'"[3]

The **MTD** theme song would the one that goes, "God is watching us from a distance."[4] Once I attended an Orthodox dinner where a young woman performed this song. Afterward the archbishop complimented her voice, and then said he would correct the lyrics: "God is watching us from *no* distance."

Can you see what a tumult of opinions overflowed in Europe in the second millennium? And all these ideas were proposed by people who were sincere and prayerful, and who closely studied the Bible. The result is a field of chaos.

I can promise you that, when this book is published, I'll start hearing from people who complain that I didn't describe their beliefs accurately; I didn't include enough *detail*. I didn't distinguish their branch of the tree from an adjoining, similar branch. I didn't use the specific words they do, or cite the right scriptures. They'll say that there are *many* more meticulous distinctions between their theological edifice and the erroneous one next door.

And you know what? They'll be right. There is no end to the fineness of these distinctions. Adherents may boast, "Look how precise our theology is!" But viewed from the outside, such extreme detail only demonstrates how completely Western theology has been shattered. Could this possibly be God's will?

. . .

Through all those centuries, as Protestants and Catholics were wrangling and asserting new theories (and sometimes killing each other), Orthodox Christians were believing and teaching the same original, unchanged faith (and sometimes killing each other). Yes, Orthodox are as susceptible as other Christians when it comes to the temptations of property and power. But *they don't need to fight about theology*. They keep on believing and teaching the same ancient faith. Someone said, "They may not be speaking to each other, but they could finish each other's sentences." [5]

How can that be possible? Briefly: in the West, theology comes from theologians, like milk comes from cows. A theologian's job is to come up with new ideas, so new opinions keep arriving and jousting with each other.

But Orthodox theology is grounded in community memory. Each generation, within each "tribe and tongue," receives the same faith and hands it on intact. Someone who tried to update the faith would only demonstrate that he had left the community.

Orthodoxy is not the Perfect Church—there is no perfect church. But there is a True Faith. You'll find that same faith in the Orthodox church near you.

Here's my objection to the whole concept of merits. (Did I say that it's not in the Bible?) The view that Christ's merits are applied to our sins treats sin as if it were a *legal* matter. Sin is viewed as breaking a law, like going over the speed limit. Jesus pays our debt, just as a friend could give you the money for a speeding ticket.

But in the Orthodox view, sin is like a *medical* matter. Sin is *death*. To sin is to take poison and begin to die. No one could be freed from sin on your behalf, no more than a friend could endure chemotherapy in your place.

Sin becomes addiction. We cling to our precious sins, even though they are killing us. Forgiveness is not the problem here; God tosses aside every legal claim and forgives us for free. Yet the poison of sin still runs through us, in the great catastrophe of the Fall.

Salvation brings us, not only forgiveness, but also release from bondage to the misery of sin. For "the Lamb of God… takes away the sin of the world" (John 1:29). Not just the penalty for sin, but *sin itself*.

That is the promise. "Everyone who commits sin is a slave to sin. The slave does not continue in the house for ever; the son continues for ever. So if the Son makes you free, you will be free indeed" (John 8:34-36).

The Orthodox life is a long and loving process of healing, in which Christ leads and empowers us, and we cooperate the best we can. We accumulate small victories and big ones, keeping our eyes on the Cross. The friends of Christ who walked this path before us are a great encouragement.

Sometimes we vanquish sin, rising above it in triumph. And sometimes it knocks us down, or we fall down somewhat willingly, in our weakness. When that happens God picks us up, dusts us off, and sets us on our feet again. The Orthodox life is a daily struggle against sin, a struggle for the freedom that is the birthright of a son.

One more thing to note about the **Satisfaction** theory and its descendants: it has a reassuringly *transactional* basis. We already know how that works; we deal with transactions every day. So if Christ pays a debt he does not owe, and then gives his reward to us, it means God is *obliged* to forgive us.

That's an immensely satisfying idea—a "satisfaction" theory in another sense.

For we don't like to feel indebted. When we receive a gift and can give nothing in return, it makes us feel uneasy. That doesn't change when the giver is God.

I think that's one reason for the great success of the **Satisfaction** theory in Europe. It's easier to grasp the idea of a straightforward transaction than to comprehend God's vast and unreasonable love. It relieves the stress we feel over being forgiven for free, and eternally put in God's debt. It relieves the stress of being loved and forgiven for reasons we can't control—reasons wholly within God himself.

This summary of Western atonement theory is only a hop and a skip over some of the variations, and if you wanted to read further you could go on for years. The supporters of each theory can produce scriptures that, they believe, prove their interpretation is correct. Their opponents produce other scriptures that, they believe, confute the first theory and vindicate their own.

Let's admit it: *everybody's* theory is founded on the Bible. The ability to find a multitude of interpretations in the Scriptures is just what happens when a multitude of people scrutinize the same text. (Maybe you've endured this as a member of a committee to draft a mission statement.)

But these widely-divergent theories can't *all* be right, can they? Didn't the New Testament writers have something specific in mind as they were writing? Could they possibly have intended to provide a tray of words that Christians could keep rearranging, one century after another, producing innumerable opposing ideas?

As N. T. Wright points out, "To put it crudely, the Eastern

Orthodox churches never had 'an Anselm.' That alone should alert us to the possibility that some of our great controversies may have more to do with fresh interpretive schemes introduced at a later date than with the original meaning of the Bible." [6]

Nobody, no matter how brilliant, can interpret the Scriptures more accurately than the original hearers could. If a consistent way of understanding those Scriptures was identified at the start (say, by people who knew koine Greek, living in the Bible lands around the eastern end of the Mediterranean), shouldn't that get our attention?

The idea that God's honor had to be restored before he could forgive us doesn't appear until a *thousand years* into the Christian story. Such theories arose in a different era, culture, and language, and on a whole different continent, than the one the New Testament writers knew. I have seen Eastern Christians astonished and appalled when they learn that *any* Christian believes Christ died to pay our sin-debt to the Father.

Scripture demonstrates that God forgives us for free, the way we are supposed to forgive each other. He forgives us without payment, like the father of the Prodigal forgave his son (Luke 15:11–32). He does this because he *loves* us. Which brings us to the next chapter.

6

FORGIVENESS AND MERCY

To Western Christians, one of the most startling aspects of the Orthodox view of salvation is that it sees no requirements that have to be met before God can forgive us. If prior payment was necessary, then it wouldn't *be* forgiveness.

Here's what I mean. Imagine that at the end of a restaurant meal the waiter tells you, "No charge! The manager has forgiven your debt." On the other hand, he might say, "No charge! The guy at that table paid your debt."

That's the difference between forgiveness and third-party payment. God does the first; he actually *forgives* us. Forgiveness must be free, if it is to be forgiveness at all.

Yes, we owe God a great debt for our sin, a debt we could never pay. But God simply cancels the debt. It's like the man in Jesus' parable: "A certain creditor had two debtors; one owed five hundred denarii, and the other fifty. When they could not pay, he forgave them both" (Luke 7:41–42). God gives us **Forgiveness** and **Mercy**, without requiring satisfaction of his honor or repayment of our debt.

That's how we're supposed to forgive each other, isn't it? We should forgive someone who injures us without demanding restitution, or even requiring them to say they're sorry. Every time we say the Lord's Prayer we repeat the principle:

"Forgive us our trespasses, as we forgive those who trespass against us" (Matthew 6:12). [1]

St. Paul says the same:

"Be kind to one another, tenderhearted, forgiving one another, as God in Christ forgave you" (Ephesian 4:32).

"If one has a complaint against another, forgive each other; as the Lord has forgiven you, so you also must forgive" (Colossians 3:13).

This is one of Christ's most difficult teachings, and perhaps the one least put into practice, but we can't say it's complicated. Even when restitution is just and necessary, even when trust can't be restored, we are still called to give preemptive, unilateral forgiveness.[2]

But if you and I forgive each other without demanding repayment, we do the very thing that troubled St. Anselm: we treat sinner and sinless alike, we leave sin uncorrected, and we knock the scales of justice awry.

To look at it from the other direction: if God had to receive satisfaction before granting forgiveness, then "as we forgive" would mean we had to do the same. We *couldn't* forgive a serious injury, not until there was restitution or punishment. To graciously waive repayment would wreck eternal justice.

And how would we know where to stop? If serious injuries must be redressed, wouldn't non-serious ones need to be, as well? Say we were strangers on the subway, and you stepped on my foot. We'd have to figure out what it was worth (a quarter? How hard did you step?), and you would have to pay me before I could forgive you and we could get on with our day. If I said, "It's okay, don't worry about it," I would be wreaking injustice, and treating thoughtless you the same as the innocent billions who never stepped on my foot.

If we had to receive payment for every injury, we could hardly get through a day for all the confusion and aggravation it would cause. We know it is right to let some things pass without demanding that everything be paid in full. Forgiveness does not count the cost. Forgiveness is free.

Now, St. Anselm would have thought the solution to this dilemma was obvious: God's honor is infinite, but mine isn't. I learned from James Bowman's book *Honor: A History* that in traditional societies no one "would suggest that the low-born and ill-bred were as capable of honor as the nobility."[3] People in the lower classes don't even *have* honor. That belongs to the wealthy and powerful alone, and they are obligated to preserve it. So I can forgive freely, but God's hands are tied.

In *Lord, Have Mercy*, Scott Hahn presents this point of view in the context of sacramental Reconciliation (Confession) in the Roman Catholic Church. Our offenses against God are vastly more serious than those we commit against each other, he says. It is like the penalty you'd receive for punching the president of the United States, compared with the penalty you'd get for punching your neighbor.[4]

But we're not shocked when a powerful person forgives a great injury, are we? When Pope John Paul II was shot, he went to the jail and forgave the gunman. He didn't withhold forgiveness till his honor was restored—even though he held the highest honor in the Roman Catholic Church.

And this unilateral forgiveness didn't astound or offend people. Nobody complained that, by forgiving the gunman, he undermined eternal justice. Nobody demanded satisfaction for the injured honor of the papacy. On the contrary, people were moved by the beauty of the pope's action. Forgiving without repayment is not only for us peons; the powerful can forgive as well.

Jesus says, in fact, that when we forgive we are behaving like our Father. "Love your enemies and pray for those who persecute you, so that you may be sons of your Father who is in heaven; for he makes his sun rise on the evil and on the good, and sends rain on the just and on the unjust…Be perfect, as your heavenly Father is perfect" (Matthew 5:44-45,48).

So we're not shocked today if a powerful person grants forgiveness. The idea must have made sense in Christ's time too, since it's an essential plot point in the parable of the Prodigal Son. But in Anselm's time, it was a problem. He worked out the theology to solve that problem, and it took lasting hold.

When Protestants look at Orthodoxy and see liturgy and vestments, they may assume it is tainted by the "works righteousness" beliefs they ascribe to Roman Catholicism. (Leaving aside, for the moment, how accurately they understand Catholicism.) But Orthodox believe that *nothing* we do pays the debt for our sins. God simply forgives it.

> "But God, who is rich in mercy, out of the great love with which he loved us, even when we were dead through our trespasses, made us alive together with Christ (by grace you have been saved)...[that] he might show the immeasurable riches of his grace in kindness toward us in Christ Jesus. For by grace you have been saved through faith; and this is not your own doing, it is the gift of God–not because of works, lest any man should boast" (Ephesians 2:4-9).

God the All-Powerful forgives us because of a motivation inside himself: the "great love with which he loved us." Nothing we do can block the impulse of that love. We can ignore it, fight against it, or blaspheme it; we can shrug it off and voluntarily unite ourselves with Death. We can send ourselves to Hell any way we want. But we can't stop God from forgiving us. He forgives us the way we're supposed to forgive each other—for free.

St. Isaac of Syria, a seventh-century bishop of Nineveh, points out that we can't call God just, in human terms, since he pays the laborers who worked only one hour as much as those who worked all day, and the father of the prodigal embraces his son without any restitution. "Do not call God just," St. Isaac says, "for his justice is not manifest in the things regarding *you*." [5]

What kind of love does God have for us? When we're trying to understand God's love, it's best to think about how a parent can love a child, even an angry, rejecting child. Ezekiel gives us this heartbroken cry:

"As I live, says the Lord God, I have no pleasure in the death of the wicked, but that the wicked turn from his way and live. Turn back, turn back from your evil ways; for why will you die, O house of Israel?" (Ezekiel 33:11).

Christ taught us to call God "Our Father," and gave us a story to demonstrate what a father's love is like. When it begins, the younger son in the family is already a vortex of resentment and disdain. He asks his father to give him his share of the estate, which would be his upon his father's death. It was the equivalent of saying, "You are dead to me." Then the son turned on his heel and left, and he didn't go off a few blocks to pout. He immediately set out for "a far country," putting as much space as possible between himself and his father.

This father no doubt knew his son well. It was probably not the first angry outburst. As the son packed his goods and headed off, the father watched him go. In that desert, treeless land, he could follow this angry son with his eyes, watching as the figure got smaller and smaller in the distance, till it finally disappeared.

The father watched for a long time. The next day he brought out a chair, and he watched some more. He kept watching. Day after day went by. One day he saw a tiny figure, far away on the horizon. It was his son, coming home.

"While he was yet at a distance, his father saw him and had compassion, and ran and embraced him and kissed him" (Luke 15:20). This father wasn't concerned for his honor, or even his dignity. Though his son had given him a deadly insult, he ran to him and caught him up in an embrace. The son didn't even get a chance to make his little "I was wrong" speech; the father was already giving orders for the welcome-home feast.

In another version of the story, the father might have said, "I'd love to take you home, son, but who's going to pay this Visa bill? Somebody's got to pay the debt first."

Or he might have said, "I'd love to take you home, but I can't have people thinking I would overlook an insult. I'm going to have to punish you, for the sake of my honor."

Or he might have said, "I'm so full of wrath I can't see straight. Even if I killed you, it wouldn't be enough. You're not worth killing. You're garbage. But your older brother, who has never offended me—he is innocent. I'll kill him, and the sight of his blood will soothe my wrath."

The older brother doesn't always get a fair shake, when people talk about this parable. He has a legitimate complaint: the younger son has squandered his half of the inheritance, and from now on they'll all be living on the elder brother's share. It *isn't* fair, to tell the truth. When the father welcomes back the prodigal without requiring repayment, it is unjust, in earthly terms. But the father invites the older son to sacrifice his legitimate claim, and join him in a love that doesn't count the cost.

The relationship between Christ's sacrifice on the Cross and the forgiveness of our sins has been understood in many different ways over the last millennium. I think the most straightforward is the one we see in this parable, this very memorable story that touches all hearers deeply.

We see the penitent son and the father's joy, and we see the elder brother invited to let go of his just claims and join in. Their reconciliation will be marked by a joyous banquet.

The fatted calf is the costly sacrifice that is the center of the feast, which sets a seal on their reunion. It is the father who provides the calf.

7
SACRIFICES AND OFFERINGS

The fatted calf played a role in the banquet that was more than merely nutritious. It was the festive centerpiece of the meal, the kind of delicacy you'd keep in reserve for a special occasion. The roasted calf would be the centerpiece in a literal sense, as the family gathered around the table to eat from a common dish.

The fact that this is an *expensive* sort of entrée is significant. The costliness of the father's sacrifice sets a seal upon the reunion in a way an ordinary meal could not.

The really important moments in life are often marked by lavish meals and ceremonies, and the giving and receiving of gifts. Picture the rulers of two ancient lands coming together to seal a covenant. The host will receive his guest with lavish hospitality, and the visiting ruler will bring forth impressive gifts. Significant gifts are appropriate to the making of a covenant, because they demonstrate the depth of each partner's commitment.

In the sacrificial system of the Old Testament, covenants with God were "ratified with blood" (Hebrews 9:18). We see this in Exodus 19, when God invited the Hebrew refugees to "be my own possession among all peoples" (Exodus 19:5). Oxen were sacrificed, and Moses threw the blood on both the altar and the people (Exodus 24:6-8), uniting God and his chosen ones through the sprinkling of blood. This is "the blood of the covenant which God commanded you" (Hebrews 9:20).

Notice that, on that ancient occasion, the sacrifice was not being offered for *sin*. It was offered to seal the great covenant between God and his people.

For the next fifteen centuries, the Hebrew people continued to make many kinds of sacrifices: freewill offerings, peace offerings, thank offerings, and gifts in fulfillment of vows, in addition to offerings for sin. Every offering was a re-affirmation of the original covenant between God and his people.

And then, at the turning point of time, the old covenant was concluded and a new one began. "This cup is the new covenant in my blood" (1 Corinthians 11:25).

Jesus Christ is the ultimate offering of the human race to the Father, the final offering for sin. As St. Paul says, "Under the law almost everything is purified with blood, and without the shedding of blood there is no forgiveness" (Hebrews 9:22).

But, Paul continues, animal sacrifices were not sufficient, and never could be: "It is impossible that the blood of bulls and goats should take away sins" (Hebrews 10:4). He then ascribes to Christ the words in Psalm 39/40:6–8:

> "Sacrifices and offerings you have not desired,
>   But a body you have prepared for me;
>   In burnt offerings and sin offerings you have taken no pleasure.

> Then I said, 'Behold, I have come to do your will, O God,
>
> As it is written of me in the roll of the book.'" (Hebrews 10:5-7).[1]

When Christ takes on the body the Father has prepared for him, the futile, repetitive shedding of animal blood is brought to an end. Now "we have been sanctified through the offering of the body of Jesus Christ once for all" (Hebrews 10:10).

Christ's death on the Cross was an offering to the Father —but it wasn't a payment. This is a distinction we don't readily catch, because the making of sacrifices is no longer a feature of daily life. But it was never the case that the Father needed animal blood before he could forgive his people. It was rather that his people needed to *offer* it. Sinners needed to make a costly gift as evidence to themselves and others that they were sincere; they needed to show that they really were sorry for their sin, and really intended to renounce it.

Gifts have no power of coercion; an offering can't compel a penitent sinner to live righteously. But a gift sets a seal on his *intention*. The Temple sacrifices and offerings demonstrated a commitment to God and an intention to live righteously. They never were *payments* for sin.

This can be rather a new thought, if we are used to thinking of salvation as a transaction: a big pile of debt on this side, and a big pile of payment over there, and now we're in the clear. I think what leads us astray is that we think the Old Testament sacrifices were like the offerings made in the old Greco-Roman religion, which went to pay off debts or win divine favors. That's rather a crass idea, and unworthy of attribution to the God-guided Hebrew people.

No, our relationship with God doesn't have a legal or financial character. It is a relationship of love, like that of parent and child, and love functions under different rules than law and finance do.

For example, love "does not keep account of wrongdoing" (1 Corinthians 13:5). Love doesn't keep track of how many sins there are, and sit back with arms folded until it is paid off. Love doesn't worry about who owes what. When it starts fretting about being cheated or not getting a fair shake, it has stopped being love.

Yet love does give gifts, sometimes very costly gifts, as a seal and proof of commitment. Think of a man who wants to give his fiancée an engagement ring. The ring does not have the character of a contract or legal obligation; he is not buying the girl from her family, or bribing her away from them. The size of the diamond has no literal correspondence to the size of his love.

Yet it is appropriate that the ring be costly *to him*. It is right that the purchase be something of a sacrifice for him, because it stands as a visible proof of his love, to his beloved and to all the world. Love wants the world to know.

Here's another indication that sin offerings were not payments: if they were, every sin would have had its own objective cost, no matter who the sinner was. The price tag on Sin X would always be the same for everybody, rich and poor.

But Scripture provides instead that the amount of payment could vary according to what the person can afford. Leviticus says that someone who has sinned must bring a lamb as a sin offering, "but if he cannot afford a lamb, then he shall bring, as his guilt offering to the Lord for the sin which he has committed, two turtledoves or two young pigeons" (Leviticus 5:7).

If the same sins have different price tags, the sacrifice is not a payment or transaction. Instead, it's a gift. But the giver needs to *feel* it to be a sacrifice; it needs to feel like a stretch. Each sinner needs to give the offering that is a sacrifice *to him*.

That kind of flexibility does not constitute justice. If a poor person and a rich one commit the same sin, their debt is objectively the same. But the point of an offering lies in the act of giving. It's giving that heals a relationship, and the face value of the gift is beside the point. When you come to a new depth of relationship and want to mark it with a gift, that gift should really cost you something.

On the founding of his new covenant, Christ offered himself to the Father as the representative of the whole human race; he was the offering of immeasurable cost that we gave to the Father. God gave us a costly gift as well: the blood of his beloved Son, and with it the forgiveness of our sins. On both sides, human and divine, the exchange was of a gift, an extraordinary and ultimate gift, not a transaction.

These gifts seal the new covenant between God and humanity: "In Christ God was reconciling the world to himself, not counting their trespasses against them" (2 Corinthians 5:19). Notice that St. Paul says "*not* counting their trespasses;" he does not say God counted the trespasses, weighed the Cross, and considered the debt well paid. The purpose of the sacrifice is reconciliation, not repayment.

If you knocked over a vase and broke it in a museum, you'd be in trouble with an institution; you might face various penalties for the damage you'd done. But if you knocked over a vase and broke it in a friend's house, you'd have harmed your friend. The harm was direct and personal, rather than institutional. You'd urgently want to repair the relationship, and would start with a heartfelt apology. If instead you asked the price of the vase and wrote out a check, it would only make things worse.

In the Old Testament, God makes it emphatically clear how little interest he has in the sacrifices themselves. He's looking for penitence and gratitude, and even the costliest sacrifice can't substitute for that. A sacrifice for sin should reveal how deeply you repent of that sin, and making the sacrifice without repentance is not just meaningless, but insulting. God shows contempt for such empty gestures:

> "I hate, I despise your feasts....
> Even though you offer me
> your burnt offerings and cereal offerings,
> I will not accept them" (Amos 5:21–22).

Imagine a faithless husband who keeps cheating on his wife, and every time she finds out he tries to smooth things over with a gift of expensive jewelry. The day will come when she will throw it in his face. A gift that expresses deep repentance is a beautiful thing, even if it isn't expensive. But a gift that is insincere and manipulative is insulting, no matter what its cost.

The further absurdity of such a gift is that God already owns everything. He even gave us the Christ that we offer back to him. An insincere offering is like that callous husband who, instead of buying his wife something new, takes a bracelet out of her jewelry box and wraps it in new gift paper. To sin and then try to buy God off with something he already owns—something you can get your hands on only because he put it in your keeping—is as insulting as it is ludicrous.

> "For you have no delight in sacrifice;
> were I to give a burnt offering,
> you would not be pleased.
> The sacrifice acceptable to God is a broken spirit;
> a broken and contrite heart, O God,
> you will not despise" (Psalm 50/51:16–17).

A sincere and penitent heart, even if it can give no gift, is sufficient. Penitence with a gift, a costly gift, is a good and fitting thing. But a gift without penitence is garbage.

Sacrifices and **offerings** are the way God ordained, in his ancient conversations with Moses, for his people to renew their covenant with him. Yet it was all too tempting for them —as it would be for us, no doubt—to treat the arrangement as a transaction. It would be comfortable to think that, if you did something wrong, all you had to do was slap a sheep on the altar and you'd be in the clear. You wouldn't need repentance; you wouldn't need humility, or self-knowledge, or a moment of painful honesty. You wouldn't need humble gratitude for God's mercies. All you'd need is a sheep.

You can almost hear our Lord's frustration as he says, "Go and learn what this means, 'I desire mercy, and not sacrifice.' For I came not to call the righteous, but sinners" (Matthew 9:13).

. . .

The one who came to call sinners would himself bear their sin, like a lamb sacrificed in the temple ("Behold the Lamb of God, who takes away the sin of the world!," John 1:29). We're so used to those words that it's hard for us to grasp how inherently shocking it is. The tendency of human nature to think of sacrifices as payments—give a sheep, get forgiveness—is upended when God breaks into human life and provides his own sacrifice on our behalf. This was foretold by the prophet Isaiah:

> "Surely he has borne our griefs
> and carried our sorrows;
> yet we esteemed him stricken,
> smitten by God, and afflicted.
> But he was wounded for our transgressions,
> he was bruised for our iniquities;
> upon him was the chastisement that made us whole,
> and with his stripes we are healed.
> All we like sheep have gone astray;
> we have turned every one to his own way;
> and the LORD has laid on him the iniquity of us all."
> (Isaiah 53:4-6)

Under the new covenant, we come to God offering his Son, our Lord Jesus Christ, as the sacrifice for our sins. God, in return, grants us forgiveness, and in this way the covenant is forged. But *God gave us his Son in the first place*. He didn't require that we give an adequate sacrifice before he would accept reconciliation; he himself provided the sacrifice, one we didn't even know that we should offer. God himself completed the terms of this new covenant, and St. Paul urges us to accept this invitation:

TWO VIEWS OF THE CROSS 49

"All this is from God, who through Christ reconciled us to himself…[I]n Christ God was reconciling the world to himself, not counting their trespasses against them…So we are ambassadors for Christ, God making his appeal through us. We beseech you on behalf of Christ, be reconciled to God. For our sake he made him to be sin who knew no sin, so that in him we might become the righteousness of God" (2 Corinthians 5:18-21).

"Since all have sinned and fallen short of the glory of God, they are justified by his grace as a gift, through the redemption which is in Christ Jesus, whom God put forward as a *hilasterios* [mercy-place] by his blood, to be redeemed by faith. This was to show God's righteousness, because in his divine forbearance he had passed over former sins" (Romans 3:23-25).

(Note that Paul says he *passed over* our sins; he doesn't say God required payment for them, and arranged to pay himself.)

"God has done what the law, weakened by the flesh, could not do: sending his own Son in the likeness of sinful flesh and for sin, he condemned sin in the flesh, in order that the just requirement of the law might be fulfilled in us, who walk not according to the flesh but according to the Spirit" (Romans 8:3-4).

I find it especially poignant to picture the seriousness with which the faithful sacrificed lambs in the Temple. Ever since the time of Moses, lambs had been offered in acknowledgement of sin, in a ritual marked with fitting solemnity.

But when the Lamb of God was sacrificed for the sins of

the whole world, those who took his life didn't do so with reverence. They did it with raucous levity, insults, and blows. They didn't handle him with the respect they would have given a sacrificial sheep. Our salvation comes so *completely* from God that it wasn't even necessary for the humans involved to behave with humility, penitence, or dignity. It all comes, a free gift, from God.

The **Sacrifices** and **Offerings** aspect of salvation is simple and direct: it is the restoring of a relationship of love. It's not necessary to add an extra layer of offending abstract justice, and God being unable to forgive us until that's repaid.

But if you've always arranged your mental furniture around that extra bit, it's hard to get it out again. It's fairly easy to expand, elaborate, and proliferate, when busy with intellectual matters, but it's not so easy to recover an earlier simplicity. That's one reason it takes converts a few years to get the hang of Orthodoxy.

Certainly, it's possible to interpret these Scriptures differently, and claim that they prove objective justice has to be satisfied, or a penalty paid, before God can forgive us. People can interpret any verse of Scripture in a number of ways, and each new interpretation can eventually become a venerable tradition.

But it's worth asking: When did that tradition begin? How recently did it appear, in Christian history? How closely does it resemble the understanding of the New Testament's original audience? If nobody thought of this interpretation for a thousand years, doesn't that make it kind of iffy?

We can ask further: does this interpretation lead to spiritual health? Does it create in us a lively mix of repentance and gratitude? Does it lead us into a more sure and accurate awareness of God's presence? Or does it lead us to think of God as the corresponding party in a formal transaction—all we have to do is slap his Son on a Cross, and we're in the clear?

I sometimes hear people say that we should use *all* of the theories of the atonement, because each one supplies something essential to our understanding. I can't agree completely, because the early-church belief that God forgives freely isn't compatible with the later theory that he had to be paid. Yet there is much beauty to explore in the scriptural language of **Sacrifice** and **Offering**, once it's liberated from the overtones of a one-for-one transaction.

You will hear some of that beauty if you attend Orthodox services in Holy Week. These numerous services look at Christ's suffering and death from every possible perspective, and explore dozens more Old Testament parallels than most of us ever noticed. These services are heartfelt, profound, and expressed in exquisite poetry. And you'll sometimes hear our Lord praised for taking the penalty our sins deserve.

Saying that, I feel like I'm putting the car keys into the hands of a teenage driver. What you'll find is that this idea is not pressed home in a literal, transactional way. It's one of a great profusion of thoughts that well up from our hearts, as we stand at the foot of the Cross.

The idea that *is* sustained literally, repeatedly, and emphatically is that Christ "trampled down Death by death." By his voluntary death, Christ got into Hades and defeated our ancient enemy. He suffers like a hero.

N.T. Wright says he once "had the temerity" to ask an Orthodox bishop how his church views the Cross. With a "beaming smile," the bishop said, "It is the prelude to the

Resurrection." Wright kept trying his question from different angles, but could get no other reply. ²

The Cross is a victory. It is the way to Paradise. "It is the prelude to the Resurrection."

Let's look again at the three directions of biblical language that we set out in Chapter 1. Salvation is a **Rescue** action whereby we are redeemed from the captivity of sin. The Father **Forgives** us freely, as the father in the parable forgave his prodigal son.

There remains this third aspect, threaded through Scripture in the language of **Sacrifices** and **Offerings**, in which the Son offers himself and the Father receives the offering. And yet it was always the Father who gave us his Son (John 3:16), as he had provided the ram for Abraham's sacrifice (Genesis 22:8) two thousand years before.

The rigor and solemnity of the system of sacrifices was set before the children of Israel to teach what gifts mean within a relationship of love, and how very great love can make possible the greatest of gifts: "Greater love has no man than this, that a man lay down his life for his friends" (John 15:13).

8

WHO RECEIVES THE "RANSOM"?

But what about that word, "ransom?" Scripture says, "The Son of Man came...to give his life as a ransom for many" (Matthew 20:28, Mark 10:45). What does that mean?

In the Christian West the word "ransom" is often confused with the concept of sacrifices and offerings; "ransom" is understood to mean Christ's paying our sin-debt to God. But when there's a kidnapping, the ransom doesn't go to the chief of police. We didn't need to be redeemed or ransomed from God. The Father was not holding us captive.

The problem is that our understanding of the term "ransom" has narrowed over the centuries. When we hear the word, we picture a big bag of money with a dollar sign on it, the kind well-appointed bank robbers carry in cartoons.

But it used to mean doing whatever was needed to set someone free. You could "ransom" or "redeem" someone in a number of ways. You pay for their freedom—satisfying the kidnapper's demands, or paying the slave-owner's price. Or you could offer to take the person's place, becoming a slave or hostage yourself. Or you could just help the captive escape.

That last is what God did when he freed Israel from Egypt. He didn't pay Pharaoh anything, or demand payment for himself. He just reached out and did it with his "mighty hand" (Deuteronomy 9:26).

In our story of the kidnapped teens, the brave young officer "ransomed" or "redeemed" them out of captivity by breaking down the door and helping them run free. He "ransomed them by his blood," because he freed them at the cost of his own life.

When townspeople say of that officer, "He paid for those kids' freedom with his blood," someone who didn't understand English very well might say, "Who did he pay?" Did he trade the kidnappers a little vial of blood in return for the kids' freedom? Or did he give his blood to the police chief? (And how would that free the kids?) No, they'd explain, it's a figure of speech. Nobody actually *received* any blood. It was a courageous, self-giving act, but not a bargain or transaction. The officer "gave his blood" in the sense that he willingly died; the result was that the teens were freed.

This most ancient view of salvation is often called, by Western theologians, the **Ransom** theory. They set it alongside the theories that emerged in the West a millennium later, the **Satisfaction** and **Moral Influence** theories, and the rest. But *ransom* has become a misleading term, since it's now taken narrowly to mean paying for someone's release. In contemporary English, "ransom" no longer indicates the possibility of setting captives free by a mighty, courageous deed. When we hear "ransom," we picture that big bag of money.

So I call this the **Rescue** theory, since that term echoes most clearly the deliverance of God's people at the Red Sea, the primary Old Testament event that foreshadows the Cross. "Rescue" is just my own term; Orthodox Christians simply call it "salvation," for there are no other theories.

The understanding of salvation as a rescue action was reintroduced to the West a century ago, by the Swedish Lutheran archbishop Gustaf Aulén (1879–1977).[1] He called this view *Christus Victor*, which is the title of his well-regarded book.

Aulén makes the point that, though we call this the **Ransom** (or **Rescue**) or **Christus Victor** theory, it isn't a fully worked-out theory; it doesn't attempt to tie up all the loose ends. The earliest Christians were sure that that Christ's suffering, death, and Resurrection freed them from Death, but they didn't venture to spell out exactly how it worked. Yet they went confidently, willingly to their deaths in the Roman persecution, armed with this belief alone—not even a full-fledged "theory" but simply an "idea" of the atonement, in Aulén's view.

You sometimes encounter in the early Fathers' writings a theme that, by becoming incarnate and dying, Christ *tricked* the devil; Hades gulped down his human body, and was exploded by his divinity. The Syrian hymnographer St. Romanos the Melodist (AD 475–518) wrote a song-sermon depicting an argument between the evil one and gluttonous Hades, who has devoured all the dead from the beginning. In this somewhat-humorous dialogue they gaze upon the Cross, and the evil one keeps boasting about his great triumph. But Hades isn't sure he agrees; his stomach doesn't feel so good.

The evil one deceived by Christ's human disguise is a theme some early authors enjoyed; the devil was tricked like a fish into swallowing a baited hook (St. Gregory of Nyssa[2]) or like a mouse taking the bait in a trap (St. Augustine[3]). In that sense Christ could be seen as offering to the evil one a *decoy* ransom, like that money-bag filled with counterfeit bills and a dye pack.

But no church father proposed that the devil received a *genuine* ransom in return for our freedom. The devil didn't deserve such payment; even if he did, Christ would have taken it back when he rose from the dead.

We can see an aspect of justice in this view of salvation, in that God acted *fittingly* toward the devil in setting us free. As All-Powerful, he could have simply swept away the consequences of human sin. Instead, he sent his Son to share in our human nature, to live and die as one of us. The evil one took the bait, seizing not a sinful man but a sinless one, and lost everything as a result. Justice was served, for God beat the devil fair and square.

To anyone who interpreted "ransom" as a literal payment, St. Gregory of Nazianzus (AD 330–339) warned that the analogy cannot be pressed. "To whom was that blood offered, that was shed for us? Since a ransom belongs only to him who holds in bondage, I ask to whom this was offered?"

To the devil, perhaps? But it would be outrageous for the evil one to receive "ransom, not only from God, but ransom which consists of God himself." The devil, a murderer and liar from the beginning (John 8:44), had no right to any payment.

St. Gregory goes on, "But if [the payment is] to the Father, first I ask, How? For it was not by him that we were being oppressed. And second, why should the blood of the Only-Begotten delight the Father, who would not receive even Isaac when he was being offered by his father as a sacrifice?" If God would not receive the offered blood of Isaac, why would he be pleased with the blood of his beloved Son?

St. Gregory sums up: the Son offers himself as a sacrifice to honor the Father; the Father accepts this sacrifice without having demanded it; the final result is the defeat of the evil one. "This is as much as we shall say of Christ; the greater portion shall be reverenced with silence."[4]

In the end, there is little we can comprehend about these things. This was a battle fought over the children's heads. All we need to know is that we have been rescued; we are free, safe, and loved.

9
DEPICTING THE CRUCIFIXION

These distinctions between the views of salvation, East and West, are evident in the different ways the Crucifixion is depicted. Perhaps the most resoundingly impressive depiction of the Crucifixion in recent years would be the 2004 movie, *The Passion of the Christ*.

The Passion featured scenes that were extensively bloody, which shocked many viewers and aroused some controversy. But news stories explained that, although depictions of the Crucifixion were restrained in the early centuries, that changed around the time of the Black Plague (14th century). Since people were seeing horrific suffering on every side, artists were inclined to portray the Cross more realistically. You can see an example of such a depiction on the right side of the cover, painted by Hendrick Ter Brugghen about 1625.

Depictions of the Crucifixion in the West have continued to evolve ever since, and by now have taken almost every form imaginable. (I once saw a purple teddy bear with a Crucifixion embroidered on its tummy.) And yet the depiction of the Crucifixion in Orthodox iconography has continued to be fairly restrained.

Turn the page and we'll compare an icon of the Crucifixion, painted in the 1300s, with the Hendrick Ter Brugghen painting. These images also appear on the cover of this book.

The crucified Christ fills the center of the icon, with his head bowed in death. On the left, the Virgin Mary weeps, a frail, heartbroken old woman. On the right, St. John bows his head, bewildered and sad.

At some point in this icon's 700-year history someone gouged out the eyes of all these figures, even those of the two angels overhead. Christ's face also bears long scratches, and a zigzag of slices run up his right forearm to his hand. He is already crucified, but that's not enough for those who hate him. "By his stripes we are healed" (Isaiah 53:5), and those stripes never stop coming.

But notice something else about the way Christ is depicted in the icon. He doesn't look as if he is *suffering* on the Cross. He's not sagging from the nails in his hands, but stands on the foot platform, graceful and strong. He seems almost to be holding the Cross up, displaying it to us, as if there was a message there we could read. His arms are spread and hands are open, in the ancient stance of prayer: "Lift up your hands to the holy place, and bless the Lord" (Psalm 133/134:2).

Now look at the Ter Brugghen painting. Here Christ's body is gray-green, and with its sagging abdomen looks believably dead. (Some artists actually used cadavers as models.) Fresh, red blood streams from every wound. This is a broken Christ.

But the body of Christ in the icon is golden, and he wears, not a crown of thorns, but a halo. Only faint traces of blood appear at the nails in his feet (and probably at his hands as well, though they have been gouged away).

This golden Christ is not a beaten, defeated man. He looks, rather, like the God-man who ascended the Cross by his own will, and turned it into a throne. He is a heroic man who has accomplished his literally Death-defying mission. His facial expression is composed, even tranquil. "It is finished" (John 19:30).

Why would there be such a difference? Why is Christ portrayed heroically in the East, yet in the West is depicted in extreme suffering?

It's reasonable to say that the inescapable sights and smells of the Black Death could have impelled this shift. That grim reality, visible on every side, might have inclined artists to graphic, even gruesome, portrayals.

But medieval Europeans weren't the only Christians who saw death in terrible forms. Crucifixion was only one of the ways Romans thought up to execute people. Emperor Nero had Christians tied to poles, covered with tar, and set on fire, to serve as torches for his garden party. He had Christians bound and wrapped in bloody animal skins, then set out for dogs to eat. And there was worse.

Recurring persecutions throughout the Roman Empire made sure Christians saw, and suffered, death in cruel and grotesque ways. And yet their art kept depicting Christ as heroic rather than battered.

As icon scholar Leonid Ouspensky noted, the Roman catacomb frescoes show Bible heroes, like Daniel and the Three Young Men, not in terror and suffering, but in steadfast prayer. Those who went to visit the graves of loved ones, who would view these images, he says, didn't need to see any more suffering. They needed to see how a follower of Christ bears up under such circumstances, and that they themselves should pray and trust in God at all times. Ouspensky wrote, "That which could calm, strengthen, and teach was portrayed, and not that which could possibly repel or frighten."[1]

Perhaps Christ was depicted as serene and undefeated in the East because persecuted Christians needed that strengthening sight; perhaps he was depicted in gruesome suffering, a thousand years later in the West, because people enduring the Black Death had different needs. But surely Anselm's new theory of how we are saved had something to do with it.

The ancient Orthodox understanding of the Cross is that Christ went heroically into the depths of Hades and destroyed its power; he rescued us and set us free. The Father forgives our sins without satisfaction, payment, or penalty. Christ offers himself to the Father as a sacrifice, not a payment.

But Anselm's Satisfaction atonement theory begins with the assumption that the Father *couldn't* forgive us until his injured honor was satisfied. Christ died on the Cross and restored that honor, then turned his due reward over to us.

If you believe that Christ's suffering paid our debt to God, then it is fitting for it to look brutally violent. Our sins are overwhelmingly evil and numerous, and we would be helpless before such debt. The awful extent of Christ's suffering shows us the awful extent of our sins. From that perspective, we need to see Christ primarily as a sufferer.

By contrast, the glorious Christ in the icon is majestic and powerful, even in death. Undoubtedly, he suffered on the Cross, but icons don't depict him in agony. They show him as our rescuer, the great hero of our salvation story.

How do we depict heroes?

Let's return to my (imperfect) story of the rescued teens. The brave officer's sacrifice made a big impression on the townspeople, and they decided to put up a statue in his honor. How will they want to portray him? He endured torture, humiliation, and death to set their children free, and that moves them deeply. But would they want the statue to depict that—to show him enduring the full horror of those hours, broken and bleeding?

No, of course not. It is his *victory* they want to proclaim. The pain he suffered increases their gratitude all the more, but prying into the details seems disrespectful. The townspeople want to protect his dignity, and draw a curtain over that hideous scene. The statue of the officer will show him as they think of him, courageous and strong.

Now imagine that a movie director comes to town, and says he wants to make a film about that brave officer. To the townspeople, that sounds like a great idea. But then the director explains that he particularly wants to focus on the torture. He wants to linger over the officer's debasement and humiliation, with plenty of gore.

The townspeople would find that idea repulsive. They would consider it insulting to the hero they admire.

The Gospel writers were artists as well, employing words rather than paint. They too faced the decision of how to depict the Crucifixion. The evangelists could have dwelt on it at length, if they wanted; there was no lack of information about that cruel form of execution, and eyewitnesses of Christ's Crucifixion were still alive. With such resources at hand, how did the Gospel-writers describe Christ's suffering?

Even though these four authors write in different styles and emphasize different aspects of Christ's life, they all made same decision: when they came to the Crucifixion, they described it as briefly as possible. Matthew, Mark, Luke, and John say, "They crucified him,"[2] and provide no further details.

These authors weren't ignorant of the facts of crucifixion. They weren't inclined to conceal that the Lord had died a criminal's death; St. Paul, writing even earlier, proclaimed that he would glory in nothing but the Cross (Galatians 6:14). Nor did they avoid the gory details out of a general inclination toward daintiness. St. Luke, the most polished of the four writers, describes Judas's death in graphic terms (Acts 1:18).

And yet, when they came to the part of the story where the Lord of Glory suffers and dies, each of them observed a discreet silence. It is fitting, at such a moment, to turn our eyes away.

On the afternoon of Great and Holy Friday (Good Friday), Orthodox worshippers assemble for a Vespers service. They take the icon of Christ's body down from its wooden Cross, wrap it in white linen, and the priest places it upon the altar. Then we sing this memorable hymn:

> All Creation was changed by fear
> When it saw you hanging upon the Cross, O Christ.
> The sun was darkened
> And the foundations of the earth were shaken.
> All things suffered with the Creator of all.
> O Lord who willingly endured this for us,
> Glory to you.

All Creation was shaken with fear at seeing its Creator's self-emptying, his humiliation "unto death, even death on a Cross" (Philippians 2:8). Icons sometimes include, in the sky behind the Cross, the sun and moon turning away, and distraught angels covering their eyes. When a hero is being broken by evil, we quickly look away.

A work of art that focuses on the pain and blood presumes that we can empathize with Christ's suffering; we can know what it felt like. But a work that draws back in awe assumes that we can have *no idea* how it felt; we cannot begin to comprehend it. When God comes to suffer and die, all we can do is bow down in awe.

Earlier I said that bloody presentations of the Crucifixion are more "realistic." But what was reality, on that Good Friday? A graphic depiction could show only the reality that was visible to human eyes; it would look the same for those who mocked Christ as for those who mourned him.

An icon, on the other hand, shows a deeper reality, the one that only believers can see. In that reality, our Lord was victorious on the Cross. It was there that he won his victory over Death, our ancient enemy.

Are we able to see that reality? Much of the work in spiritual growth is along that line; we are always trying to adjust our perception so we can see the "real" reality, crashing through the assumption that we are independent beings, and God is somewhere else, too busy to notice what we're doing.

But if "even the hairs of your head are all numbered" (Matthew 10:30), God is thoroughly aware of our every deed, our every thought. Though we drift along distracted, God is already present within every moment. It's good to get used to that idea, because it's the truth. Even if we pass through our familiar world like sleepwalkers, God is *everywhere* there, thoroughly and intimately present.

The kind of realism depicted in icons helps correct our foggy perception. It sets us in line with the presence of God throughout all Creation, mightier than the forces that heave up mountains, and closer than a sigh. We need to see victorious images of the Crucifixion—in fact, need to see Christ's victory in every icon—precisely because our grasp of reality is so fragmented and weak.

10

SIN AND RIGHTEOUSNESS

We have talked a great deal about salvation without talking about its target: sin. So let's step back in time, before St. Anselm and his **Satisfaction** atonement theory, and think about sin itself.

"Original Sin" is a foundational concept in Western Christianity, developed by St. Augustine of Hippo (AD 354–430). St. Augustine proposed that, because Adam and Eve fell into sin, every person is born with a broken human nature that inclines her to sin.

That's not a view unique to St. Augustine, of course; it's also held by Orthodox Christians, and is common Christian belief just about everywhere. Even those who take Adam and Eve as symbolic characters regard their story as conveying something true about our human condition.

But St. Augustine developed a corollary to his theory. He taught that every human being is born, not just disposed to sin, but already *guilty* of sin. We all share in Adam's guilt, simply because we share in human life. Only Catholic baptism can take away the stain of sin, he said; without it, even nice people go to Hell.

The hard case that challenged St. Augustine had to do with babies who die before they are baptized. If they are guilty of Adam's sin even before birth, do they go to Hell? St. Augustine had the courage of his convictions, and said yes, such children were condemned and excluded from Heaven (though, he said, they would experience "the mildest condemnation of all."[1])[2]

Eastern Christians have never believed that we are born already guilty of the sin of Adam and Eve, so where did the idea come from? This is one of those odd moments in history, where big things turned on a single word.

As St. Augustine read his Bible in Latin translation (as we noted before, he didn't read Greek well), he came to a verse that contained an ambiguous preposition. The verse is Romans 5:12, and in the Greek original St. Paul says, "Sin came into the world through one man, and death through sin; and so death spread to all men, because all men sinned." The syntax is a bit convoluted, but in short it says: sin came into the world through Adam; sin produces death; so death has spread to everyone, because everyone sins.

But as St. Augustine read his Latin Bible he saw, not "*because* all men sinned," but "*in whom* [that is, in Adam] all men sinned". He read this passage as stating that all the members of the human race sinned "in Adam;" we all participate in Adam's sin. Augustine reasoned that we must therefore also share in his guilt. As the New England Primer of 1690 put it, "In Adam's Fall we sinned all."

Orthodox value St. Augustine's devotional writings, but are more selective when it comes to his theology. (And not his alone; there's a saying: "100% of the Church Fathers are right

80% of the time.") We recognize that every person, in fact all Creation, has been damaged by the Fall. (We don't call this by St. Augustine's term, "Original Sin," but speak instead of "Ancestral Sin.") Still, we are all born in innocence. We don't bear guilt for our sins until we are mature enough to take responsibility for our moral decisions. Children eventually begin going to confession along with their parents, but the Church doesn't assign an expiration date for childhood innocence.

Though East and West have historically disagreed on whether all humanity inherits Adam's guilt, we do agree that we receive and pass on a brokenness that inclines us to sin, and through sin to death. But did you ever wonder *how* it is passed on?

St. Augustine, considering the problem with some literalness, thought that it was transmitted in the act of reproduction, as evidenced by lust.[3] "Insofar as [Christians] are the children of God, they do not beget in a carnal manner. . . . [Christians who do] become parents, beget children because they have not yet put off the entirety of their old nature." He could not have foreseen children conceived *in vitro,* without sex, but their passionless conception probably does not render them incapable of sin.

There hasn't been a sense of urgency among Orthodox to specify the mechanism by which this susceptibility to sin and death is passed on, but rather a general perception that we share some things simply because we are all part of the same human family. We are one in a common life, so the disease of sin runs through us all. When Adam and Eve broke God's law, they simultaneously broke his Creation, and we inherit that condition and pass it on, rolling from one generation to the next.

. . .

But you know what's odd about that, to me? That we have never gotten used to this. Everybody knows that *something is wrong*. Every religion recognizes that something is wrecked, in the world and in our lives. You don't have to be a professional philosopher to notice this; a shepherd on a hillside could compose a psalm that expresses it poignantly.

Yet we don't just accept it, as we do so many other regrettables in life. Some days it's going to rain; some little league teams are going to lose. I have to stand on a kitchen chair to reach the top shelf, but I don't really *grieve* over being five feet tall. We don't wage futile, tearful battle in our thoughts over the injustice of not being able to fly, or to leap about in time, or to turn into a graceful giraffe. We simply accept the great majority of limiting or uncomfortable conditions we find within and around us.

But the sickness of sin, which causes evil people to do heinous things, and even the less evil to gravely damage themselves and other people—that is something we never quite get used to.

Once after I'd given a talk on Orthodox spirituality, an audience member asked me why Christians put so much emphasis on sin and repentance. Why not do as she'd learned at a Buddhist retreat, and simply accept that this is the way we are? Why not drop the word *sin* and practice "radical acceptance"?

In reply, I didn't have to say, "Because sin offends God." It's more than sufficient to note that sin offends *us*. We couldn't *bear* to just accept the evil in the world. We somehow know we were made for more than this. It's like we're born with a memory of something we've never seen. We yearn to return to a place we've never been. We mourn that loss and seek it every day, no matter what our religion, or none.

It might seem odd to call that general dysfunction "sin." In Western theology, sins have traditionally been thought of as specific, deliberate actions. In the Roman Catholic Church a great deal of thought went into defining when someone becomes guilty of a sin—what, exactly, constitutes (these are technical terms) "culpability," and when a sin is "imputed."

In that Church, a sin is classed as *mortal* only if it fulfills three criteria: it must involve a "grave matter," the person must have had "full understanding" of the sinfulness of the act, and he or she must have done it with "deliberate consent." If one or more of those factors are missing, the deed might be classed as a lesser, *venial* sin, or possibly not involve culpability at all. The Catholic Catechism says, "Unintentional ignorance can diminish or even remove the imputability of a grave offense."[4]

This concept of sin fits well with the idea of atonement we've been discussing, that a sin amounts to breaking the law; justice, or God's honor, must be satisfied before forgiveness can be bestowed. Thus, sins are distinct, wholly intentional, objectively wrong actions, which could theoretically be repaid by a third party.

For Orthodox Christians, it's more serious than that. Sin is instead the vast condition of brokenness and corruption pervading Creation on every side. We are born with a fatal weakness for sin, and embrace it, and die. It is a corruption of the soul, an illness that feeds on itself and consigns us to Death. We suffer from sin, and also inflict it; we perpetuate it with the fearful, selfish things we do and say and think.

. . .

This is one of the most significant differences between Western and Eastern Christian theology:

In Euro-American Christianity, **"the wages of sin is death"** (Romans 6:23) means that the *punishment* for sin is death. It's like saying that the punishment for speeding is a fine.

But in Orthodoxy, **"the wages of sin is death"** means that sin *is* death. The two are inextricably enmeshed: sin causes death, and fear of death causes sin.

As Scripture says:

Christ "partook of [human] nature, that through death he might destroy him who has the power of death, that is, the devil, and deliver all those who through fear of death were subject to lifelong bondage" (Hebrews 2:14-15).

"Sin when it is full-grown brings forth death" (James 1:15).

"You he made alive, when you were dead through the trespasses and sins in which you once walked" (Ephesians 2:1-2).

Because sin separates us from God, it separates us from life, light, love, and every good thing. To sin is to absorb death within your mind, within your feeble body.

Death is the *result* of sin, not a punishment. It is a consequence. A mother who tells her son, "If you keep climbing up there, you'll fall and break your leg," and is proved right, didn't inflict the broken leg as a punishment.

Our sins hurt not only those near us, but contribute to the wrecked, off-balance condition of all Creation. We suffer from it as we do from breathing polluted air. We may feel like we are solitary, independent actors when we sin, but our choices inevitably reverberate through the lives of others.

The radio humorist Garrison Keillor told a story that illustrates this interconnection. It concerns a man who is tempted to commit adultery, but on reflection sees how one act of betrayal can unbalance an entire community.

I saw that we all depend on each other. I saw that although I thought my sins could be secret, that they would be no more secret than an earthquake. All these houses and all these families, my infidelity will somehow shake them. It will pollute the drinking water. It will make noxious gases come out of the ventilators in the elementary school. When we scream in senseless anger, blocks away a little girl we do not know spills a bowl of gravy all over a white tablecloth.[5]

We would be helpless in this mess, without Christ's intervention. He came, not just to defeat Death but to begin our healing, the refashioning of the human race, to free us from this deadly cycle.

11

INTENTIONAL AND UNINTENTIONAL

There's something else about sin, though. We can contribute to the world's burden of sin *unintentionally*. Perhaps you once said something in a conversation that you later learned had hurt one of the hearers very much. You would deeply regret the pain you caused. Even though you didn't mean to, even if it was only in a small and transient way, you nevertheless added more weight to the world's burden of darkness and grief.

This, too, is sin. It's inevitable that we will make unintentional mistakes, and it's right that we are sorry for them, even if, under the above conditions, we would not technically be "culpable."

And what about all the times you hurt someone, and *didn't* find out? How often we hurt people by not noticing them, or not remembering them, when we intend no hurt at all. The hurt is exactly that: the person wasn't important enough to us to remember. And let's not get started on the times that, in some sneaky corner of our hearts, malice *was* mixed up in what we "unintentionally" did or didn't do.

The Lord knows all about it when I flounder in such sins, even when I manage to keep my own awareness vague. He knows me well, and the evil one does, too, and my closest friends and family have a front-row seat. The only one left out of this information loop—the only one with a sunny impression of my all-around niceness—is me.

All of that jumble of pain is sin. Whenever we contribute to this deadly smog, we participate in sin, even if we didn't intend to, or didn't know it was a sin. As Orthodox say in a prayer before receiving Communion, "Have mercy upon me and forgive my transgressions, both voluntary and involuntary, of word and of deed, of knowledge and of ignorance."

It sounds strange to ask forgiveness for sins that were involuntary, or even unknown; by the definition in the Catholic Catechism, above, we would not be culpable for unintentional sins. But if you caused a friend some hurt or pain without meaning to, of *course* you would be sorry. Of course you would ask him to forgive you, once you realized that you'd hurt him. You'd also be sorry that you had added *any* more pain to the burden of this weary world.

So culpability is not the point. You wouldn't say of a friend you'd unintentionally wounded, "He might be hurt, but that doesn't concern me. I didn't do it on purpose." With a friend, it's all about keeping a relationship in good repair. It's the same in our relationship with God.

You might think that this much broader definition of sin would so greatly increase our sense of guilt that we would collapse under the weight. But it has the opposite effect: it sets us free—free to be powerless, and cling to nothing but the Cross. We are enmeshed in sin simply because we "bear flesh and live in the world," as a Holy Week prayer says. We can't escape it, and our hearts are crooked enough to perpetuate it in ways that don't even rise to awareness. But we're absolutely forgiven, and begin each new day with valor and determination.

We have some help in this. Christ "takes away the sins of the world" (John 1:29); not just the penalty for sin, but the *sins themselves*. He gives us the great gift of forgiveness, then gives us even more, teaching us how to resist temptation, delivering us from the slavery of our chaotic and conflicting desires. For sin is brutal slavery: "[E]very one who commits sin is a slave to sin...[I]f the Son makes you free, you will be free indeed" (John 8:34-36). Christ comes to set us free. And we come to him like the sick and blind, who begged him for healing.

There's a distinctively challenging quality to the Orthodox spiritual life, and it's evident in this call to vigilance about sin. A practical result is that, in the daily life of Orthodox Christians, there's something to *do*. There are battles to be won or lost, battles that have eternal consequences. Converts often comment on the invigorating nature of this, and appreciate its challenging tone. That's particularly so if their previous experience as a Christian was that, after "making a decision for Christ," there was nothing to do. You just while away the time till you can die and go to Heaven.

Scripture presents us instead with a forthright challenge to battle temptation and overcome sin. There's no trace of the idea that salvation is a single decision, and after that you just try to be nice. On the contrary, Christ is emphatic about the need to really struggle against sin:

"Unless your righteousness exceeds that of the scribes and Pharisees, you will never enter the kingdom of heaven" (Matthew 5:20).

"Be perfect, as your heavenly Father is perfect" (Matthew 5:48).

"Not everyone who says to me, 'Lord, Lord,' shall enter the kingdom of heaven, but he who does the will of my Father who is in heaven" (Matthew 7:21).

"Blessed…are those who hear the word of God and keep it" Luke 11:28).

The Apostles agree:

"Since we have these promises, beloved, let us cleanse ourselves from every defilement of body and spirit, and make holiness perfect in the fear of God" (2 Corinthians 7:1).

"For we are his workmanship, created in Christ Jesus for good works, which God prepared beforehand, that we should walk in them" (Ephesians 2:10).

"I therefore, a prisoner for the Lord, beg you to lead a life worthy of the calling to which you have been called" (Ephesians 4:1).

"Strive … for the holiness without which no one will see the Lord" (Hebrews 12:14).

"As he who called you is holy, be holy yourselves in all your conduct; since it is written, 'You shall be holy, for I am holy'" (1Peter 1:15-16).

There are two kinds of people in the Kingdom of God: the righteous (those who actually manage to lead God-pleasing lives) and, far more numerous, repentant sinners, who delight the angels even more (Luke 15:7). In an Orthodox anecdote, the devil disputes with the Lord over the soul of a fallen, but Christ-loving, sinner. The Lord settles the argument by saying, "This is my property, and I am taking it in the condition in which I find it."

But even though repentant sinners abound in Paradise, there's no role for *unrepentant* sinners. Penitent sinners find that our struggle against sin changes and strengthens us, no matter how often we lose. It is the struggle itself that is transformative. It is what we really are, and not a legal fiction, that will encounter the Light of Christ when this life ends. It's what we have actually made of ourselves that will be "tested by fire" (1 Peter 1:7). A claim that we have put on purely-theoretical, externally-applied righteousness will be no more helpful in that encounter than 3-D glasses at a solar eclipse.

This great emphasis on resisting sin might be associated elsewhere with anxiety about being holy enough to get into Heaven, or doubts about whether the debt for sin has been fully paid. That's not the case here; Jesus has already borne our sins, dying as the sacrificial offering that seals the new covenant, and revealing himself as our champion and deliverer. God has already forgiven us, "passing over former sins" (Romans 3:25). Those sins have been wiped away, but we must still do battle with present and future sins. We must grow stronger, because sin is so tangled up with death.

God always loves and forgives us, but we are always free to turn away and choose sin instead. If we do, we will find next time that our choice is not as free; our souls are weaker and our desires are stronger. Continuing in this way will damage and confuse us more and more; we can reach a point where we no longer care about God, and have no desire to be saved.

So we take warning from the example of Judas who "cast away his salvation in a single night" (from an Orthodox hymn for Holy Week).

We don't treat our past sins lightly; they cost the life of God's Son. It's useful to ponder them, because that helps us learn where our weaknesses lie. When we repent, all our past sins are forgiven; but we face a battlefield ahead, where our souls will ultimately be won or lost.

12
HADES, FIRE, AND THE EVIL ONE

In all these discussions of Western theories of the atonement, the devil didn't come up. These days, bringing him up sounds quaint or superstitious. But you have to wonder how he came to disappear, considering how often he's mentioned in the New Testament.

Jesus takes the existence of the devil for granted, and many of his healings include a deliverance from the evil one's power. The literal, malevolent presence of the evil one is such a staple fact in the New Testament that it's puzzling that so many contemporary Christians (even those who insist they're thoroughly biblical) *don't* find room for him in their beliefs.

My hunch is that this disappearance was an unanticipated side-effect of the **Satisfaction** theory. Recall that under the **Ransomed, Redeemed, Delivered,** and **Saved** heading the evil one fills an essential role in the story: the devil is who Jesus rescues us *from*. The story wouldn't make any sense without the devil as the antagonist.

But in St. Anselm's theory, all the action takes place between the Father and the Son. The Son restores the Father's honor, the Father owes him a reward, and the Son bestows that reward on us. The devil isn't necessary to that story.

While researching this book, I read many web pages that advocated the idea (descending from the original **Satisfaction** theory) that Jesus paid the debt we owe to God for our sins. Sometimes I'd do a search for the word "devil" on those pages, and it virtually never appeared.

Yet there are some 140 references to the devil in the New Testament. Jesus taught us to pray specifically for protection from the devil: "Deliver us from the evil one" [1] (Matthew 6:13).

The people of Anselm's time didn't immediately eliminate the devil from their beliefs, of course. But, in time, the devil's role in the story began to fade. He got reduced to the role of an extra, standing at the edge of the stage with his tail and pitchfork, while the Father and the Son got all the lines.

There's another reason belief in the devil continues in the Orthodox Church: direct personal experience. The spiritual warfare that is a continuing theme in the New Testament has never ceased. As St. Paul reminded the Ephesians, "We are not contending against flesh and blood, but against the principalities, against the powers, against the world rulers of this present darkness, against the spiritual hosts of wickedness in the heavenly places" (Ephesians 6:12).

I shouldn't have to say this, but the evil one is really *evil*. Don't picture him as an amusing caricature, trying to tempt a fat lady to eat more chocolate. Picture the most hideous story you've ever heard of torture or child abuse. In the very worst of it there is a flash of glee. That's his fingerprint.

When we consider the presence of evil all through the world, all through history, in all its many guises, the concept of the devil becomes rapidly less funny. Orthodox would say that the evil we see in the world comes not only from the brokenness of Creation, not only from human sin, but also from the deliberate, malicious work of demons, intelligent beings that hate the human race.

The existence of demons is a common belief worldwide, appearing in many religions. Most people, in most times and places, have believed in the existence of evil spirits. Even those who scoff at such ideas can usually recall a time they felt a mysterious unease, or sensed a disturbing presence hanging about a place or even a person. We might be picking up such spiritual perceptions pretty regularly (positive ones, too, of course), but they don't rise to conscious awareness, because we think we don't believe in that stuff. That stuff could be real, all the same. It doesn't care if you believe in it.

You might wonder why I keep referring to "Hades" rather than "Hell." Technically, Hell—the "lake of fire" (Revelation 19:20)—doesn't exist yet.

When we come to the end of our earthly lives, death rips body and soul apart. The friends of God then dwell in Paradise ("Today you will be with me in Paradise," Luke 23:43), while those who "loved darkness rather than light" (John 3:19) dwell in Hades. [2]

Our sojourn in Paradise or Hades is temporary, though, because we were created as embodied beings. At the Final Judgment there will be a resurrection of all human life, and we will be restored to our bodies, in some unimaginable form.

(Truly unimaginable. Both Jesus [John 12:24] and Paul [1 Corinthians 15:37-8] use the analogy to a seed turning into a plant: a seed is buried in the ground, disintegrates, and then puts forth a green and living plant that looks nothing whatsoever like the seed.)

At the Resurrection of all the departed, we will enter a re-embodied life in a "new Heaven and a new earth" (Revelation 21:1). Those who love God will dwell with him in Heaven, while those who reject him will suffer in Hell.

But at present, in the interim between Christ's Resurrection and the Last Judgement, the departed abide in Paradise or Hades. Those terms are misleading, since neither is a place, in a geographic or even spatial sense. When you're beyond space and time and no longer inhabit a body, insisting on a specific valley outside Jerusalem as your destination is being overly literal. But we who know no other form of existence find it difficult to discuss the topic without using the preposition *in*, and envisioning separate locales.

The terms "Heaven" and "Hell" point toward the same all-encompassing thing: the blazing, fiery light of God's love. So let's think for a minute about the properties of light, because we tend to miss an important aspect of its meaning in the Scriptures.

Until modern times, the only source of light was fire—whether an oil lamp, a cooking fire, or the blazing midday sun. So any time you see a reference to *light* in an ancient text, you should remember that the author expected you to picture *fire*. When the Bible says, "God is light" (1 John 1:15), we shouldn't think of a table lamp. St. John had something more dangerous in mind.

In every land and every time, respect for fire was one of

the first lessons children learned. Used wisely, fire is a blessing; it gives light and warmth, cooks food, cheers the soul. But carelessness or misuse can be catastrophic, leading to searing pain, destruction, and death.

Fire will not change its nature, but we will be changed by fire, to our good or loss, depending on how we approach it. "Our God is a consuming fire" (Deuteronomy 4:24; Hebrews 12:29). When you're dealing with fire, you should respect its properties and approach it wisely. "The fear [reverent awe] of the Lord is the beginning of wisdom" (Psalm 110/111:10).

Reflecting on the nature of fire helps us understand how the presence of God could be joy to some people and pain to others. We will all spend eternity in God's presence; we are in his presence now, but it is veiled by Creation. In the next life, the veil will be taken away. What will that unveiled presence be like?

Someone who loves God will find that all-pervading light to be life and joy, and fully comprehend at last that "God is love" (1 John 4:8, 16). But one who "love[s] darkness rather than light" (John 3:19) will find the inescapable light misery and destruction. This light will become to him paradoxical darkness, an "outer darkness [where] people will weep and gnash their teeth" (Matthew 8:12; 22:13; 25:30).

But if God is offering us his love, some ask, how could it feel like pain? A friend told me the story of how, as a child, he went with his mother to give a Christmas gift to an estranged aunt. First the mother opened a gift the aunt offered, and found something insultingly cheap. She thanked her, and offered her own gift. When the aunt had unwrapped it just enough to see that she'd been given something lovely and valuable, she exploded in rage; she shouted, "You did that on purpose!"

Even in this life, for some people, love burns. And God is always love. He is always light. He is always fire. People can experience that presence in very different ways, depending on whether they welcome or defy him.

13
THE PROBLEM OF EVIL

A discussion of the evil one brings us to the topic of evil itself. Western Christianity has done a great deal of painful struggling with the "problem of evil," the question of why there is suffering in the world, the suffering of the innocent in particular. It could be said that this is the single most significant, and most unanswerable, religious issue there is. Atheists certainly love to bash believers with it. They ask: How can God let an innocent person suffer? We draw a blank, and that lack of an answer points in the chilly direction of doubting the goodness of God.

But after I had been Orthodox for some years I noticed that this question just wasn't coming up. Orthodox Christians suffer as much as people anywhere, of course, and experience just as much tragedy and loss. But they don't compound that pain with worries about God's goodness or power. Apparently, they thought of this as a question that has an answer.

One part of the answer is to think, when we see suffering, "I did this." Because all human life is one, because we all swim in a common sea, I helped cause this, with my heedless, selfish sins. I helped pollute the world, and make it the kind of place where things like this can happen. Like air pollution, the fog of sin hurts everyone who breathes.

But there is another element of that answer. As Jesus said, "An enemy has done this" (Matthew 13:28). There is a malevolent agency that savors and exploits the evil we do. By our sins, we cooperate with him and increase his power.

And of *course* he will use that power to make the innocent suffer. He loves to see suffering, and when the victim is a helpless child, it's even more delicious. For him, that's a twofer: he gets to enjoy the spectacle of suffering in those who should least have to bear it, and he gets to enjoy the anguish that we, the less-innocent, feel as we helplessly look on. The fact that such events grieve and trouble us delights him all the more; there's even a chance it could destroy our faith.

This is one of the ways we bear the burden of our sins, from the terrible pain we feel when we see the innocent suffer—and knowing that our sins help make this the kind of world where things like that can happen.

But to the devil, human suffering is only a delightful bonus; his real goal is to alienate us from the Lord. His strategy is *temptation*. That doesn't mean only things that give us pleasure; he is just as likely to tempt us toward fear, self-hatred, or despair. Anything that turns us away from the Lord will serve his purpose.

The thing to remember about temptation—the great

insight in Orthodox spirituality—is that it starts with a *thought*. A thought passes by, and we notice it, and then engage with it, and by gradual steps keep going until we put it into practice. With habitual repetition the process becomes a slip-n-slide, with hardly breathing room between the initial suggestion and collapse.

> "Each person is tempted when he is lured and enticed by his own desire. Then desire when it has conceived gives birth to sin; and sin when it is full-grown brings forth death" (James 1:14-15).

The cure for falling into sin is not berating or hating yourself, and certainly not thinking that God despises you. Technically speaking, God is never disappointed in us; his expectations weren't that high to begin with.

Our goal is to learn how to resist temptation, but desperate attempts at iron willpower can produce frustration and disappointment. What's needed is watchfulness—in Greek, *nepsis*. Since temptation begins with a thought, we need to start noticing the thoughts that appear in our minds, that weave around and through, seeking a weak spot. The idea is to notice them *early*, and shut them off. Block them before they get stronger and harder to resist.

Here's how you do that. There's a part of your mind that *watches your mind*. There's a part of your mind that's like a little island, where you notice your thoughts as they come and go. There you can evaluate them, and decide whether to take them up or turn them away. Everybody has this little island; it's the place where, when you have a stupid idea, it tells you, "That's a stupid idea."

The habit of regular prayer can expand and strengthen

that inner place, and you will discover that the Lord is standing there beside you, as you watch all that comes and goes. As your strength and discernment increase, you become able to recognize a distracting or distressing thought while it's still in the distance, and deflect it.

It's helpful, in cultivating this mental habit, to keep a favorite scripture or short prayer in mind (perhaps the ancient Jesus Prayer, which goes, "Lord Jesus Christ, Son of God, have mercy on me"). That way, when you want to turn away from a troublesome thought, you've already established something to turn to. A positive and profoundly true thought, a sincere prayer, becomes a kind of home base, and you can turn to it instantly instead of following a destructive thought.

Tempting thoughts, no matter how loathsome, should not distress us; they may not even be our own thoughts, but just missiles flung at us by the evil one in his attempts to drag us away. So just let them pass. There's a saying, "The birds fly overhead, but you don't have to let them nest in your hair."

And don't get pulled into trying to debate or refute them. Any kind of engagement with a thought can pull you into a downward slide. Just recognize them when you see them, and turn back to your constant inner prayer. "Rejoice always, pray constantly, give thanks in everything, for this is God's will for you in Christ Jesus" (1 Thessalonians 5:16-18).

Over the centuries, the psychology of temptation has been thoroughly mapped by Orthodox athletes of prayer, and the tactic of simply dismissing those thoughts and turning prayerfully toward Jesus has proved to be the best strategy. It accords with our Lord's many exhortations to vigilance, and his parables about the wise virgins (Matthew

25:1-12) and the watchful householder (Luke 12:39). "What I say to you, I say to all: Watch" (Mark 13:37).

St. Peter wrote: "Be sober [*neptic*], be watchful. Your adversary the devil prowls around like a roaring lion, seeking someone to devour. Resist him, firm in your faith" (1Peter 5:8-9).

The Scriptures consistently call us to resist the evil one, and we should take his existence seriously—but it's dangerous to become fascinated with demonic or supernatural manifestations. That can open the door to all kinds of things beyond your control. You wouldn't know what you were dealing with, and you wouldn't have the upper hand. Just try to stay in command of your thoughts. And keep turning back to Jesus every time, asking for his help and mercy.

The trivializing of all these topics—the devil, Hell, sin, temptation—has rendered us mostly defenseless against them. We should reflect that these concepts weren't invented by some comic Southern preacher, but come from the pages of the Bible. Jesus himself used the phrase "fire and brimstone,"[1] and repeatedly spoke of those who will suffer eternally in fire.[2]

Even though it's a fire, it's also a place of darkness, a place of isolation, "where there will be weeping and gnashing of teeth" (a description Jesus emphasized with multiple repetitions).[3] If we can't piece together those different descriptions, we can at least recognize that they convey nothing so clearly as suffering. Suffering which is as much emotional as physical; the pain of loneliness and alienation from all that is safe and good, from all that is beautiful.

The pain of being a speck in a cold universe with no boundaries, falling forever in emptiness, out of touch with light.

And God is the opposite of that—not cozy warmth, but brilliant light that burns through everything to clarity, and orders all reality in its course. The idea of God's "kingdom" is a weak earthly analogy for the unimaginably vast authority that underlies the universe. All of Creation is his, and he governs every atom, every star. And the energy of it is love.

14
MERCY AND REPENTANCE

"Lord have mercy" is something Orthodox Christians say frequently during worship—once after each petition in an intercessory litany, or sometimes three times, and in a few Lenten services we say a hundred in a row. Newcomers can find this unsettling. Why do we have to keep begging God to be merciful? Is he really that bad-tempered? It sounds like a criminal begging a judge for a lighter sentence.

But lots of people in the Gospels asked Jesus for mercy, and none of them were seeking leniency. What they sought was his compassion.

The Syro-Phoenecian woman begged for her daughter to be freed from a demon, saying, "Have mercy on me, O Lord!" (Matthew 15:22).

The ten lepers cried, "Jesus, Master, have mercy on us!" (Luke 17:13).

Blind Bartimaeus kept shouting "Jesus, Son of David, have mercy on me!" (Mark 10:47), even though everyone was telling him to be quiet.

These petitioners weren't begging a judge to let them off easy. They were people who knew their need, and cast all their hopes on Jesus.

We, too, say "Lord, have mercy," reminding ourselves that he is merciful and all-powerful, and that he will hear us just as compassionately as he heard them long ago. The Greek *Kyrie eleison,* "Lord, have mercy," resonates with the word for olive oil, *elaion,* the medium for healing balm. (The good Samaritan cared for the beaten man's wounds, "pouring on *elaion* and wine," Luke 10:34.)

"Lord, have mercy" contains all those meanings, yet there's a strain of penitence, too. It is appropriate, when we ask for Christ's help, to recognize how poorly we reciprocate his kindness. Every day we contribute our share of garbage and confusion to the world's dysfunction. So when we come to God in prayer, we stand beside the tax collector in Christ's parable, who "would not even lift his eyes to heaven but beat his breast, saying, 'God, be merciful to me a sinner!'" (Luke 18:13).

The many repetitions in Orthodox worship of "Lord, have mercy," the many references to sin and repentance, help keep us from trusting in ourselves, and train us in self-skepticism. But they also continually remind us that God *is* merciful, and faithful in his love. We are striving always to hold two things in balance: sorrow over our weakness before sin, and joy at God's all-transcending love.

There's a pattern seen among the great saints, East and

West, that those who ascend the highest are the most aware of their sins. They consider themselves worse sinners than anyone else; St. Paul said, "I am the chief of sinners" (1 Timothy 1:15).

Why would they feel that way? One reason, no doubt, is that the closer you get to the light, the darker your shadow appears. But I think something else is also going on, that has to do with hurting someone we love.

Remember when you knocked over that vase, at your friend's house? That heirloom vase her grandmother gave her? Think about the way her face looked: initially an expression of shock, even horror—but that was quickly followed by an attempt to rearrange her features, to keep you from feeling terrible. She started saying reassuring things, like telling you that it wasn't really that valuable, even though shock lingered in her eyes. Nevertheless, her love for you overruled her sorrow. She valued her friendship with you more than any old vase.

Whenever that awful memory replays in your mind, you can see those changes in your friend's face. It is visible proof that her love for you was greater than any pain you caused.

I think that experience would leave you with two simultaneous impressions. You would first feel a fresh pang of sorrow every time you think of how you hurt her, knowing how much she loves you; and, second, you would feel a fresh astonished joy every time you think of how much she loves you, in light of how much you hurt her. Those two things link together, around and around: the severity of the pain you caused her is the very thing that reveals the depth of her love.

I think that's why the great saints, who might seem to us nearly sinless, keep becoming more penitent as the years go by. It's because with every sin they realize more deeply the extent of the damage they've caused themselves and others; and, by the same token, they realize more clearly the extent of God's love. Deep penitence keeps producing deep joy.

St. John Climacus (AD 525–606) coined a word for it: *charmolypi*, which combines two Greek words to mean "joy-making sorrow." As you advance along the way of prayer, this becomes a naturally-occurring state. Sorrow over sin ushers in great joy, accompanied by gratitude and an increasing sense of freedom.

When you become *utterly* convinced of God's love, you're convinced that his love precedes and follows and surrounds every moment of your life, past, present, and future. There is nothing that he can't forgive—nothing that, in terms of your eternal salvation, he hasn't already forgiven. If you're deeply convinced of that, when a guilty memory surfaces, you don't panic, blame self, blame others, spiral downward. The memory arises into a place completely irradiated with God's love. You think, "You loved me then, too. You were forgiving then, too."

There comes a sting of regret—"How ungrateful, how selfish I was, when God loves me this much"—and then a flood of gratitude. You realize that God's love is even greater than you ever knew. Sorrow releases great joy.

One at a time, your bad memories have their teeth pulled in this way. Finding repentance is like finding a vein of gold in a mountain, and following it into ever-deepening joy.

We Christians are always telling each other that our faith is not about rules, but about a relationship—our relationship with God, who loves us. Those words can sound pretty flat, though. It all sounds so hypothetical—like some faraway, invisible God is having pleasant thoughts about us.

The truth is that he is right here with us, *within* us, and his love is sustaining everything we see, every minute. It is only by his love that we take the next breath.

But we won't be able to grasp or know that love if we think of it as a distant bundle of nice feelings, and ourselves as nice people who *deserve* to be loved. God's love seems theoretical until we grasp, personally, how much he has forgiven us. "Her sins, which are many, are forgiven, for she loved much; but he who is forgiven little, loves little" (Luke 7:47).

St. Isaac of Syria (d. AD 700) thought that the pain of Hell would be caused by realizing, at last, how much God loved us, and that we have rejected his love:

> Those who are punished in Gehenna are scourged by the scourge of love. ... I mean that those who have become conscious that they have sinned against love suffer greater torment from this than from any fear of punishment. For the sorrow caused in the heart by sin against love is sharper than any torment that can be. ...This is the torment of Gehenna: bitter regret. But love inebriates the souls of the children of Heaven by its delectability.[1]

15

FREE WILL AND ASSURANCE OF SALVATION

One of the prayers in the Vespers service includes the line, "We do not seek help from any human power, but we call upon your mercy, looking confidently for your salvation."

What does "looking confidently" mean, when it comes to salvation? For many Protestants, "assurance of salvation" is a central doctrine. Some go so far as to say "Once saved, always saved": once you have accepted Christ as Savior there is *nothing* you can do to lose your salvation, even if you tried.

Orthodox seek instead to balance two truths. On the one hand, it is sobering to recall that we will one day die, and every sin will be revealed before Christ's judgement seat. On the other hand, our Lord loves us more than we can ever comprehend, and has already accomplished everything necessary for our salvation.

However—on yet another hypothetical hand—even though God is always faithful, we are not. We dare not trust too much in our own strength, or our ability to resist temptation. As St. Paul says, "Let anyone who thinks that he stands take heed lest he fall" (1 Corinthians 10:12).

The Desert Father Abba Xanthias said, "The Thief on the cross was justified by a single word; while Judas, who was counted in the number of the apostles, lost all his labor in one single night, falling from Heaven to Hell. Therefore let no one boast of his works, for all who trust in themselves fall."

I've heard Orthodox people say "Salvation is a process." That's not quite right, because you wouldn't be deprived of salvation if you died soon after you became a Christian, and hadn't had time to make much progress. Salvation isn't a process; salvation is a gift. But *life* is a process. We have to keep on making the decision to follow Christ, over and over again, day by day, and even minute by minute.

When asked "Are you saved?," a popular Orthodox response is, "I have been saved [by Christ's death on the Cross]; I am being saved [by the indwelling Holy Spirit]; I will be saved [by God's mercy on the Last Day]."

God will always love us. He chose to create us and to become our Father, and his love will continue no matter what we do. He *wants* to save us; he "desires all men to be saved and to come to the knowledge of the truth" (1 Timothy 2:4).

God will always be faithful—but we can't be so sure of ourselves. So we maintain an honest, practical humility, much like that of an addict who struggles to resist a pill or a bottle. No matter how much love there is on one side of a relationship, it is possible for one on the other side to destroy it single-handedly. Love may continue, but it is no longer a relationship.

While we have complete assurance of God's desire to save us, we remain wary of our own fickle hearts. We keep asking for mercy because we keep needing it.

. . .

The Orthodox understanding of sin applies here. There's a litany that appears in many Orthodox services, that asks for "a Christian ending to our life, painless, blameless, peaceful, and a good defense before the awesome judgment seat of Christ."

Why shouldn't we assume we'll do just fine before "the awesome judgement seat of Christ"? That would seem reasonable, if sins are deliberate misdeeds, and the debt to God has been paid.

An ordinary, nominally-Christian person, perhaps unknowingly infected with **MTD**, might think that way. He might reason like this: If a sin is akin to breaking the law, if it's like breaking the speed limit, we should assume that God will simply forgive and forget. Why would he want to punish us? Doesn't he love us? And didn't he make us with these weaknesses in the first place? If our sins are just the list of all the bad things we've ever done, any God worth the name would surely tear up the charges on Judgment Day.

But if you think of sin as sickness, corruption unto death, it's different. God hates sin like the parents of a leukemia victim hate cancer. He hates whatever hurts humankind, and sin is the miasma of agitation, selfishness, and fear that surrounds us and seeps in from every side, all through the years of this broken life.

But resisting sin is hard. If we are going to shed our cherished, habitual sins and grow in holiness, we will have to change. And we *really* don't like to change. As St. Paul accurately said, "No man ever hates his own flesh, but nourishes and cherishes it" (Ephesians 5:29). Change might mean giving up some of the things we enjoy, and when that reality begins to hit home, people can surprise themselves with how absolutely they refuse.

As we've said before, salvation is a rescue operation, as at the Red Sea. We have been freed from slavery to sin by God's "mighty hand." The Father has willingly wiped away our debt, and Christ has broken open the prison door. Now we can run to safety and freedom in the Kingdom of God.

The problem is we *keep returning to slavery*. We do this voluntarily. We cling to our sins. We are tempted to live as on a highway median—glancing backward longingly at our precious sins, calculating that we can nip back there quickly and still have time at the end to make a dash to God's side. What we don't take into calculation is that every indulgence in sin leaves us more weakened and confused.

Do we have the power to resist sin? That was a controversial question in the fifth century, when a dispute arose between the British monk Pelagius (AD 360–420) and St. Augustine of Hippo (AD 354–430). It's been a controversial question ever since, in fact, whenever sin is understood as a debt we owe to God.

The theological problem is that, if human beings are able to withstand sin by our own efforts, then we might be paying some of our own sin-debt. That would mean Christ's death on the Cross did not cover it *all*; we must contribute some goodness of our own.

Pelagius taught that humans are born free from sin, and able to choose whether or not to sin. (He said, however, that only Christ has ever *succeeded* in leading a sinless life.) Since sinful people are all we ever see, we turn into sinners as well. Pelagius thought it would be possible to live a sinless life, if we could see the example of people who were really, really good.

St. Augustine opposed this, saying that we are born with a corrupted nature, inclined to sin (Orthodox would agree), and also born guilty of Adam's sin (Orthodox would *not* agree, as we discussed in Chapter 10).

But Augustine also taught that our nature is *entirely* corrupted, and contains no health at all. Since we are corrupted in every respect, St. Augustine said, we are not able to choose not to sin. We will sin every time, unless God intervenes. (In the Protestant Reformation, this doctrine acquired the name **Total Depravity**.)

The Church, East and West, condemned Pelagius as a heretic, and regards Augustine as a saint (though no saint is perfect). But Orthodox don't agree with St. Augustine's stand against free will.

As before, your view of salvation makes a difference here. If salvation means paying the Father the debt we owe for our sins, then that payment would *have* to be entirely Christ's doing. If the Cross wasn't payment enough, we're all in trouble.

But if you look at salvation instead as a rescue action, free will has different implications. You can choose whether or not to *accept* a rescue. In that regard, you have free will. That's true, even though you don't have to do anything to *deserve* a rescue.

Picture a child sleeping in a burning house; the fireman who breaks in will rescue her, whether she likes it or not. She hasn't done anything to deserve being rescued. She doesn't even know the building is on fire. When the fireman picks her up, she might even fight hard against him, insisting that she wants to go on sleeping.

Why should we rescue this child, if she has done nothing

to merit it? Because she's a member of the human race. She's one of us. That's enough. Christ came to rescue us because the human race is uniquely his Creation. He permeates it, and his own life is the beating heart of all its life. Christ saves us because we are his; we belong to him. He stands on his rights as our Creator, rather than any merits we think we've earned.

The world doesn't know it's on fire. Christ comes to rescue us anyway. But, unlike that little girl, who will be picked up and carried to safety no matter how much she protests, we can refuse to be rescued.

We can find it very hard to give up the sins that we enjoy. St. Paul spoke for many when he said:

> I do not understand my own actions. For I do not do what I want, but I do the very thing I hate. . . I can will what is right, but I cannot do it. For I do not do the good I want, but the evil I do not want is what I do. (Romans 7:15, 18–19)

Around the time of the Augustine-Pelagius controversy, in the late 300's, St. John Cassian and his friend St. Germanus made a pilgrimage through the monasteries of Egypt and Palestine, talking with the Desert Fathers and recording their answers to difficult questions. (This collection of conversations, called *The Conferences*—in Latin, *Collationes*—was appointed to be read at mealtime in Benedictine monasteries. That's how a light meal came to be called a "collation.")

When John Cassian and Germanus came to the desert of Scetis in Egypt, they visited a number of hermits and monastic communities. They met the old abbot Paphnutius,[1] who was called "the Buffalo" because of his silence and ability to endure solitude. When they asked him about the role of free will, Paphnutius told them to look to the example of Abraham. God said to him both "leave your country" and "go to the land I will show you" (Genesis 12:1), which shows that God both calls and completes our perfection. Paphnutius said, "'The land I will show you' is not one you can discover by your own efforts, but one which I will show, not only to one who is ignorant of it, but even to one who is not looking for it."

St. Germanus then asked him, "Where then is there room for free will, and how is it ascribed to our efforts that we are worthy of praise, if God both begins and ends everything in us which concerns our salvation?"

Paphnutius replied, "This would fairly influence us, if in every work and practice the beginning and ending were everything, and there were no middle in between."

If you could arrange to keel over and die the moment you became a Christian, you'd never have to wrestle with the paradox of free will. But for most of us, there's all this middle-in-between. Every day is packed with it. Moment by moment, we are faced with decisions, shoved this way and that, compelled to make one choice after another, whether we want to or not.

Abbot Paphnutius went on, "As we know that God creates opportunities of salvation in various ways, it is in our power to make use of the opportunities granted to us by Heaven more or less earnestly." He continued,

> We ought every moment to pray . . . that he who is the unseen ruler of the human heart may vouchsafe to turn that will of ours to the desire of virtue, though it is more readily inclined to vice. . . . The Lord's help is always joined to [our effort], that we may not be altogether destroyed by

our free will, [and] when he sees that we have stumbled, he sustains and supports us, as it were by stretching out his hand.

Paphnutius begins with a situation we immediately recognize, that we regularly find ourselves confronted with moments of decision, when we can either resist sin or succumb to it. We also recognize that we respond to these "opportunities" sometimes more, and sometimes less "earnestly." And when God sees we have fallen, he reaches out to lift us up again.

A mother will not always carry her growing babies; she puts them down, because she wants them to learn to walk. God does not always carry us, his children, because we grow stronger only by testing ourselves and stretching beyond our previous successes. Sometimes our strength fails us, and we fall. It seems God has already made allowance for that. He is not at all surprised that we fell, just as a mother is not surprised when her toddler mis-steps and tumbles down.

St. Isaac of Syria (AD 613-700) wrote:

> It is like a mother who, in teaching her infant son to walk, steps back from him and calls to him. When he comes toward her on his little feet, and begins to tremble and is about to fall because of their softness and delicacy, then she runs to him and catches him in her embrace.[2]

> So the grace of God embraces and teaches those who, purely and with simplicity, have surrendered themselves into the hands of their Creator and, having renounced the world with their whole heart, follow after him.[3]

16

HOW TO TURN INTO A GOAT

It's never wise to rest comfortably on our spiritual and moral achievements, and think we can be strong in the face of temptation. We are weaker than we think we are. When we fall, we do what God expected we would do.

And so we fall, and then he stands us on our feet again, and once again we face temptation and try our strength. A little child cannot learn to walk without falling many times, and, perhaps to our surprise, God is willing to let us fall many times, and is not shocked at those failings.

Many times our feelings of guilt over sin are actually feelings of *shame*, because we expected not to fall. We thought we were stronger than that. The fall into sin astonishes and then discourages us. But the Lord knows our capabilities and our weaknesses; he knows us better than we know ourselves. And so he keeps standing us back up on our feet.

How does free will fit into this process of growth? When we're drawn toward sin, the Lord holds out the possibility of rescue, and we can choose whether or not to respond. If we do accept the rescuer's help, it doesn't mean that we earned the *right* to be rescued; he rescues us for reasons within himself, because we belong to him.

If we don't accept that help, if we refuse to be rescued, we must take full responsibility for remaining in captivity to our sins. We receive salvation as a sure and certain gift from God, yet view our traitorous desires with suspicion.

As we progress in prayer our eyes are opened again and again to how much healing we're going to need, so much more than we expected. We are always discovering anew the great extent of God's love.

A prayer in the Vespers service ends, "You do not punish us as we deserve, but abound in mercy and compassion. . . . For you are a good God and you love mankind." Many Orthodox prayers end with that thought. It seems the right balance for a faith that puts very great emphasis on repentance. Sometimes a prayer concludes, "For you alone love mankind." A startling way to put it, but true: every human love is feeble, every human love can fail. The only love worthy of the name is God's love for us.

Along with everything else God gives us, we ask him to give us strength and the will to persevere. It *all* comes from him: our rescue, his forgiveness, and our ability to endure. We are saved entirely by grace, dependent on God even for our ability to love God.

When we recognize that we need to be rescued, we put ourselves in our Father's hands. In his tender pity, and with his very precise knowledge of how we are made, he doesn't reveal to us the entire makeover plan at once. "I have yet many things to say to you, but you cannot bear them now" (John 16:12).

C. S. Lewis wrote that we think at first God is going to

turn us into a "decent little cottage," but as deep, wrenching changes continue to be made, we realize that he is building a palace. "He intends to come and live in it himself."[1]

God loves us and saves us because we are his. It's difficult for us to grasp how absolute his side of the relationship is; he loves us even while we are sinners, and nothing can halt or deflect the force of his love. He *is* love, and his love fills the universe. It comes entirely from him, and knows no limits. It takes no notice of whether we are lovable or not, whether we want him to love us or not. He will love us no matter what, and nothing can stop him.

Love so vast is hard to take in, and even makes us somewhat uncomfortable. We can't imagine what it would be like to feel that kind of love for someone else. The love we give is often impetuous, beguiled by superficial things, and if those things alter, it could fade. Familiarity alone can be enough to exhaust our enthusiasm.

God's kind of love is entirely beyond our comprehension, and that should rightly give us pause. With his vast and unreasonable love, God invites us into a recklessly self-giving relationship, with nothing held back.

Still, we are free to resist. We can go on resisting as long as we like. God is all-powerful, but the one thing over which he's chosen to cede control is what we decide to do. He created us in his image and surrounded us with bountiful Creation, and then lets us choose how we will live. The end of our life's journey will reveal what kinds of choices we made.

Making regular trips back to Egypt is a dangerous game.

Step by unseen step we could be conditioning ourselves to find God boring, and turning habits of self-indulgence into chains of addiction. We could pass a point—an unmarked point—after which we would have neither the strength nor the motivation to repent and turn one last time.

Christ said the Final Judgment will be like separating sheep from goats (Matthew 25). From Christ's description, Judgment Day is not going to be so much like a criminal trial as like a livestock show. Separating sheep from goats is one farm chore that doesn't require a lot of close scrutiny. Over a lifetime our choices will turn us into one or the other, and at the end it won't be hard to tell which one we decided to become.

When the prodigal came home, it wasn't the end of the story. He needed fresh clothes right away, and probably needed a bath, too. He was no doubt malnourished, weak from his long journey, prey to illness, infection, and parasites.

But those sorts of things would be the easiest to heal. The prodigal didn't come home because he'd suddenly had a personality transplant, but because he was desperate and had nowhere else to go. He might be just as angry as he was before, and now his pride is stung by having to accept charity. He might resent his goody-goody older brother, who firmly resents him in return. He might be embarrassed in front of the servants, who gape to see their former master reduced to such humiliation.

The Prodigal has come home, but his journey is not over. Neither is ours.

17
THE INCARNATION

As we've said, God saved us from Death for reasons within himself. We belong to him in a way nothing else in Creation does. And so he came to save us.

In my Protestant years, I thought of God's love as something we elicit from him; he found so much in us to delight him that he could not resist. Even when we feel ourselves to be unlovable, God sees our real beauty.

That's an inviting idea; certainly, we want to believe that God finds us attractive. The downside is the sneaking suspicion that God loves us this expansively only because he doesn't know us very *well*. One day this inexplicable love might encounter what we are really like, and end.

If God's motive is interior, though, nothing we do can stop him from pursuing us. He loves us because we are his.

You'll find, in Orthodox thought, the idea that God's "image" remains whole in every human being, but his "likeness" was damaged in the Fall, and by our chosen sins. As God's image, we remain ontologically and irrevocably his—

no matter how broken and distorted the likeness has become.

That's another way that God's love is like a parent's love for a child. A child may think that her parents love her because of her personal traits or accomplishments or good behavior. But her parents love her in a deep, ferocious way because she is *theirs*. They will continue to seek and rescue her, driven by this interior claim, even if she disappoints them, even if she attempts to renounce them. She is their flesh and blood, and that is a stronger claim than anything she says or does.

This understanding of God's relationship to us implies something about our relationship to each other. If we are all linked to him, then we are all linked to each other. We are united with each other, not in a merely sentimental way but *literally*, because we share a single, common life. Human life is one, and we all participate in it; each person is a rivulet from the common stream.

We are one—not just as an idealistic assertion, or even in a vaguely spiritual way, but a oneness grounded in the fact that we are all human beings. Each of us has a human body, and we all share a human nature. It's that simple. And it's a unity as real and solid as anything in material Creation.

This has implications for our salvation, for when Christ became incarnate, he began our healing. Our oneness with Adam and Eve means we are born with a fatal susceptibility to sin; but, by that same oneness, when Christ steps into our common life he sets an opposite force in motion, flooding darkness with his light.

When I was newly Orthodox, I kept asking people what early-church writings I should read to understand the

Orthodox view of the atonement. People kept telling me to read *On the Incarnation* by St. Athanasius (AD 296–373). I would say, "No, I'm not asking about the Incarnation; I'm trying to find out about the atonement" (how Christ's death on the Cross pays the sin-debt we owe to the Father). But as I read St. Athanasius's marvelously inviting treatise, I saw what they meant. Salvation is so much more than the moment of the Cross. It's the *whole story*.

Christ came, not just for our forgiveness, but to restore the human creation damaged in the Fall. St. Athanasius drew a parallel to a king visiting a city; even though he lodges in only one house, his presence bestows honor upon the whole city.

"Thus it is with the King of all," he wrote. "He has come to our realm, dwelling in one body among the many, and as a result the conspiracy of the enemy against mankind is checked, and the corruption of death is abolished." When the Son of God clothed his incorruptible nature with our human nature, "we were all surely clothed with incorruption, by the promise of the Resurrection."[1]

St. Athanasius gave another analogy: we are like a damaged portrait, for our "likeness" to God has been distorted by the pervasive disease of sin. But a damaged portrait can be restored, when the person depicted brings it back to the artist and sits for it once again. Christ did this when he "partook of [our] nature" for the sake of our salvation. "Since therefore the children share in flesh and blood, he himself likewise partook of the same nature, that through death he might destroy him who has the power of death, that is, the devil" (Hebrews 2:14).

As embodied creatures, our physicality is part of both our falling and our rising. We inherit our share in death and sin through our membership in the human race, and we received an infusion of life and healing when Christ entered the human race. "Who will deliver me from this body of death? Thanks be to God through Jesus Christ our Lord!" (Romans 7:24–25).

Since we are receiving an infusion of the life of Christ, we should expect that it will change us. Not in some emotional or vaguely-spiritual sense, nor in an external or superficial way; it changes us objectively, ontologically, a change in our very being. When Christ enters our common nature, we are united with him, just as we are united with every other human being. When we join ourselves to Christ, when we believe in him and follow him as Lord, his life flows into us like a transfusion of blood into a weak patient.

If you're used to thinking of sin as a bad deed or a broken rule, and salvation as an official pardon, these can be new ideas. If sin were only an infraction of the law, the penalty could be paid by a third party. We could then claim that payment, apply it to our sins, and be "imputed righteous." Hopefully after that we would struggle against sin and, even better, overcome it—but, technically, nothing about us *has* to change. A memorable image, supposedly from Martin Luther, is that we are like a dunghill covered with snow.[2]

But sin is infection, not infraction. It is an inward-spreading disease of the soul, dealing death to all who partake of human nature. We need to be healed, and that can't be done by changing a label.

As we noted before, Christ frees us, not just from the penalty for sin, but from *sin itself* (John 1:29). And he began that healing process in an elegantly simple way, by stepping into the flow of human life.

18

EVERYWHERE PRESENT

As a Western Christian, I thought of spirit and matter as opposites, and assumed that life in Christ meant trying to choose spiritual goods over material temptations. If asked, I would have said that God is omnipresent—but I didn't have a clear idea of what that meant. Maybe that God kept an eye on us, like a guard with a security monitor.

So, when I became Orthodox, I wasn't used to picturing God as present in my everyday world. There is an Orthodox prayer that addresses the Holy Spirit as "everywhere present and filling all things," and it kept surprising me.

Still, that echoed something I'd learned in seminary, that both classic Judaism and early Christianity saw God as present throughout Creation. Not in a merely analogical sense—"If God made this, he must be like that"—but actually permeating and pervading it. The idea is abundant in Scripture:

"Through [Christ] are all things and through [him] we exist" (1 Corinthians 8:6).

"Holy, holy, holy is the Lord of hosts; the whole earth is full of his glory" (Isaiah 6:3).

"'Do I not fill heaven and earth?' says the Lord" (Jeremiah 23:24).

"The Lord is in heaven above and on the earth beneath" (Deuteronomy 4:39).

"[Christ] fills all in all" (Ephesians 1:23).

"[The] God and Father of all...is above all and in all and through all" (Ephesians 4:6).

"[Christ] ascended...that he might fill all things" (Ephesians 4:10).

"In [Christ] all things hold together" (Colossians 1:17).

"Christ is all, and in all" (Colossians 3:11).

"In [God] we live and move and have our being" (Acts 17:28).

"Whither shall I go from your Spirit?
Or whither shall I flee from your presence?
If I ascend to heaven, you are there!
If I make my bed in Sheol, you are there!
If I take the wings of the morning
and dwell in the uttermost parts of the sea,

even there your hand shall lead me,
and your right hand shall hold me."
(Psalm 138/139:7-10)

This isn't the same thing as pantheism; the idea is not that the material world contains God, as an animist might think that there's a god inside a tree. Instead, God simultaneously fills his creation and infinitely exceeds it. Is God immanent (present in this world) or transcendent (vastly beyond it)? Trick question: he's both.

But even though this is the biblical view, you and I inherit a Christianity that has been repeatedly shellacked with dualistic Greek philosophy. We reflexively assume a stark separation between spirit and matter, and that holy things are kept in storage on the higher, ethereal level.

The view of Creation as God-saturated accounts for some other aspects of Orthodox faith, like the expectation that miracles still occur, that holy places and things are worth cherishing, and that physical disciplines, like fasting, can heal and strengthen our souls. It is why Orthodox treat the bodies of the departed with love and honor.

It's also reflected in their understanding of Holy Communion. Orthodox Christians believe that, when Jesus says "This is my Body" and "This is my Blood," that's what it is. He is God; his words create material reality, just as when he said "Let there be light."

When Orthodox Christians receive communion they are receiving Christ, in a form that will be assimilated to their bodies like any other food. (A post-communion prayer says, "Pass through me for the right ordering of all my members, my joints, my kidneys, and my heart.") The conviction that Christ is present in the Eucharist is a strong motive for the beauty and reverence of Orthodox worship.

. . .

The Bible puts it another way, saying that we are "partakers." We are partakers of:

"Grace" (Philippians 1:7)
　"The promise" (Ephesians 3:6)
　"The Holy Spirit" (Hebrews 6:4)
　"The glory that is to be revealed" (1 Peter 5:1) and
　"The divine nature" (2 Peter 1:4).

We don't merely have a relationship with God; we *partake* of him.

The idea that God is separate from our material world was so entrenched in me that it was a big thing to revise. It meant there was no longer a gap between spirit and matter—and no longer a gap between my ordinary physical life and God. That revision echoed what Athanasius said about the Incarnation, that Christ began our healing just by entering human life.

A hundred years before St. Athanasius, St. Irenaeus (AD 115–202) explored a related line of thought, saying that Christ perfected and completed everything earthly that was lost in the Fall:

> He has, in his work of recapitulation, summed up all things,[1] waging war against our enemy, and crushing him who had, at the beginning, led us away captives in Adam.[2]

Where Adam and Eve failed, Christ came in human form to retrace their steps and "recapitulate" the battle.

(Western scholars call Irenaeus's view the **Recapitulation** theory.)

In this sense, we can say that the Orthodox faith teaches a "substitutionary" view of salvation: Christ substitutes for us by representing us in the battle against the evil one, as David represented the entire Hebrew people in single combat against Goliath (1 Samuel 17). Christ substitutes for us, not to satisfy our debt or receive our punishment, but as our champion, taking our place in a battle we never could win.

St. Irenaeus goes on to say that God dealt justly with his opponent in this battle. He didn't obliterate the devil by a sweeping act of omnipotence, but instead "emptied himself, taking the form of a servant" (Philippians 2:7), undergoing our temptations, entering into our Death. Irenaeus writes:

> Indeed, the enemy would not have been fairly vanquished, unless it had been a man born of a woman who conquered him. . . . And therefore does the Lord profess himself to be the Son of Man, comprising in himself that original man [Adam]. . . in order that, as our species went down to death through a vanquished man, so we may ascend to life again through a victorious one; and as, through a man, death received the palm [of victory] against us, so again by a man we may receive the palm against death.

St. Paul expressed it simply and directly: "For as in Adam all die, so also in Christ shall all be made alive" (1 Corinthians 15:22).

19
ENERGY AND SYNERGY

Since Christ's Incarnation means his entry into human life, it means in return our entry into *his* life. The Cross defeats Death and the evil one, freeing us to turn to our Lord and take up the original work of Adam and Eve, growing into an ever-closer oneness with God.

We can go a little further to describe, though never explain, how such a relationship can be. The key terms are "essence" (*ousia* in koine Greek) and "energies" (*energeia*).

All human beings share a common *ousia*, a common human nature, characterized by traits like reason, memory, imagination, and will. This human "essence" is what unites us with each other, and distinguishes us from other living creatures.

However, each human is a distinct person (a *hypostasis*, in case you just can't get enough of those Greek terms). Each of us employs our allotment of human traits in a wholly unique way. You can't know your friend as she knows herself inside, but you can know her when you're with her and experience her "energies"—the particular ways her *energeia* expresses this *ousia* we all share.[1]

This helps us to understand the Trinity. Father, Son, and Spirit share a common *ousia*, an essence eternally beyond human comprehension. There is an inner life of the Trinity that we will never comprehend. Yet each member of the Trinity is a distinct person (*hypostasis*) and bears that common essence in a unique way.

We cannot know God in his essence (*ousia*), but we can experience and know him by his energies (*energeia*), his activity and presence overflowing in the world. By his energies, we can know him directly, and not just know about him. His energies within us empower us to do his work.

We mentioned this word "energeia" way back in Chapter 2 (when we noted that St. Jerome didn't have a Latin equivalent, so he chose *operatio*, "operation"). We have the word "energy" in English now, of course; our marvelous English language, like a magpie, picks up any shiny new word it sees. But in English bibles the "energeia" verses are translated with "operation" or "work," even though the word "energy" is sitting right there.

What might it be like, if you saw "energy" words instead of "works" and "working," in the Bible?

> "There are varieties of energies, but it is the same God who energizes them all in everyone" (1 Corinthians 12:6).

> "He who energized through Peter for the mission to the circumcised, energized through me also for the Gentiles" (Galatians 2:8).

"You accepted [the Gospel] ... as what it really is, the word of God, which is energizing in you believers" (1 Thessalonians 2:13).

"For this I toil, striving according to the energy of him energizing in me with power." (Colossians 1:29).[2]

"God is energizing in you, both to will and to energize for his good pleasure" (Philippians 2:13).

"The energizing prayer of a righteous person has great strength" (James 5:16).

"King Herod said to his servants, 'This is John the Baptist, he has been raised from the dead; that is why these powers are energizing in him.'" (Matthew 14:2).

The word "synergize" also comes to us from the Greek, and Paul uses it like this:

"We are God's synergizers" (1 Corinthians 3:9).

Timothy is God's "synergizer in the gospel of Christ" (1 Thessalonians 3:2).

When Abraham offered his son Isaac, "faith synergized his works" (James 2:22).

The disciples "preached everywhere, while the Lord synergized and confirmed their message" (Mark 16:20).

The loss of the concepts of energy and synergy were

significant for Western Christianity. Prof. David Bradshaw writes,

> If one were to summarize the differences between the Eastern and Western traditions in a single word, that word would be 'synergy.' ... For the East the highest form of communion with the divine is not primarily an intellectual act, but a sharing of life and activity. . . . [This view] led to a tendency to think of earthly, bodily existence as capable of being taken up and subsumed within the life of God. Emphasis was placed, not on any sudden transformation at death, but on the ongoing and active appropriation of those aspects of the divine life that are open to participation. . . . The underlying belief in synergy as a form of communion with God remains as clear in Gregory Palamas [AD 1296–1328] as it is in St. Paul.[3]

Yet through all this energizing and synergizing, we remain *ourselves*. Bearing God's presence doesn't make us melt away into a vast spiritual puddle. The universe was obviously created by a God who loves variety, and he made each of us closely detailed in accordance with that principle. Each person is unique and beautiful in a distinct and unrepeatable way.

Even when we enter Heaven, we will still be our unique selves. As St. Macarius of Egypt (AD 300-391) said, "Peter is Peter, Paul is Paul, Philip is Philip." Though "all become light-like, all are plunged in light and fire," they are not "turned *into* fire, with nothing of their natural substance left...[Each] remains in his own nature and personality, though filled with the Spirit."[4]

Think of the stained-glass windows in a cathedral. As you stand inside on a sunny day, you can see how distinctly each saint stands out from the others, each one radiant and unique. And yet what illuminates them is the one single light of the sun. The brighter the light of Christ becomes, the more *different* each saint appears.

Far from annihilating personality, union with God will reveal more clearly the unique person God designed each of us to be. The God whose glory "fill[s] Heaven and earth" (Jeremiah 23:24) fills us as well, and does so with patience and precision, and loving regard for our frailty.

20

THEOSIS

In Orthodoxy, theology isn't a purely intellectual undertaking; every element of the faith is there to enable our transformation. Now, at the end of the book, we come to the beginning of an extraordinary challenge, that we are called into oneness with God.

That was God's plan from the beginning. He created us in his image so we could bear his glory, just like that humble desert bush bore his fire. He placed Adam and Eve in Paradise where, in humility and obedience, they would be able to grow in oneness with him.

But our First Parents fell, and their Fall sent a crack through all Creation. Christ's Incarnation began the reversal of that damage, breaking the evil one's death-grip on us, setting us free, as Adam and Eve were free, to choose to bear God's light.

If this idea of oneness with God sounds foggy or sentimental, it's bracing to open the Scriptures and see how concrete and visible it is in practice.

One day the Lord took Peter, James, and John aside, and led them up a high mountain.

> And he was transfigured before them, and his face shone like the sun, and his garments became as white as light. ... A bright cloud overshadowed them, and a voice from the cloud said, "This is my beloved Son, with whom I am well pleased; listen to him." When the disciples heard this, they fell on their faces, and were filled with awe. But Jesus came and touched them, saying, "Rise and have no fear" (Matthew 17:1–8).

The Transfiguration did not constitute a change in Jesus; he had always been filled with glory. He just enabled his disciples to see it—temporarily, and within the limits of safety. An Orthodox hymn says that, in his Transfiguration, Christ was "revealing [his] glory to his disciples as far as they could bear it."

This event made an understandably big impression upon the three witnesses, and two of them later wrote about their time with Jesus. St. Peter retells the Transfiguration story in his Second Epistle, with the assurance that "we were eyewitnesses of his majesty" (2 Peter 1:16).

But Peter believes the Transfiguration has implications for us as well. We are supposed to share in it, and "become partakers of the divine nature" (2 Peter 1:4). Peter urges his hearers to "pay attention to this as to a lamp shining in a dark place, until the day dawns and the morning star rises in your hearts" (2 Peter 1:19).

St. John was another of the three Apostles present at the Transfiguration. He begins his intricately woven first letter with a similar claim of being an eyewitness:

"That which was from the beginning, which we have heard, which we have seen with our eyes, which we have looked upon and touched with our hands" (1 John 1:1).

He continues, perhaps thinking of that brilliant Transfiguration light:

"This is the message we have heard from him and proclaim to you, that God is light and in him is no darkness at all" (1 John 1:5).

Like Peter, John makes a connection between Christ's glory and our own destiny:

"It does not yet appear what we shall be, but we know that when he appears we shall be like him" (1 John 3:2).

Christ himself tells us that the glory he shares with the Father will be ours as well:

"The glory you have given me I have given to them, that they may be one, even as we are one" (John 17:22).

"Then the righteous will shine like the sun in the kingdom of their Father" (Matthew 13:43).

St. Paul confirms that our destiny is participation in Christ's presence and glory:

"We all, with unveiled face, beholding the glory of the Lord, are being changed into his likeness from one degree of glory to another" (2 Corinthians 3:18).

"If children, then heirs, heirs of God and fellow heirs with Christ, provided we suffer with him in order that we may also be glorified with him" (Romans 8:17).

"To know the love of Christ which surpasses knowledge, that you may be filled with all the fullness of God." (Ephesians 3:19)

This process of union with God is called *theosis*, which is usually translated "deification" or "divinization." Those terms are misleading, if not alarming, since it could sound like we expect to become junior gods, each of us an independent owner-operator of a personal divinity franchise. Fortunately for all, that is not the case.

When we dismantle the Greek word, we see that it is composed of *theos,* which means "God," and the suffix *-osis*, which indicates a process. As red dye saturates a white cloth by the process of osmosis, so humans can be saturated with God's presence by the process of theosis.

As we said, there's an Orthodox idea that fallen humanity has retained the "image" of God (that's *eikon* in Greek, "icon"), but we have damaged the "likeness" (*omoiosis* —there's that *-osis* ending again, indicating a process; in this case it's a process of "likening" or "becoming-like." To use a term only marginally less alarming than "theosis," we are undergoing a process of *assimilation*.

How does that work, though? How can humble human clay bear the overwhelming presence of God? St. Cyril of Alexandria (AD 376–444) makes an analogy to the way fire acts upon metal. He wrote, "When iron is brought into contact with fire, it becomes full of its activity"—that is, it takes on the properties of fire, its heat and light. "While it remains by nature iron, it exerts the power of fire."[1]

St. John of Damascus (AD 676–749) likewise wrote that saints "are truly called 'gods' not by nature but by participation, just as red-hot iron is called 'fire' [i.e. fiery] not by nature, but by participation in the fire's action."[2]

And St. Athanasius (AD 296–373) said it succinctly: "He was made man so that we might be made god".[3] We remain by nature human, of course, but we can "participate" in the energy and power of God.

Right from the beginning, God made us that way. Just as he gave some metals the ability to bear the heat and light of fire, he created humans, body and soul, capable of bearing his presence.

God permeates the entire material world, the whole cosmos. Everything we do, think, or say is happening in his presence. And he designed us to bear that presence, to bear his Transfiguration light, like a lump of coal bears fire.

From this perspective, we can understand why St. Paul continued to struggle against his tormenting sins, even though he put full trust in the efficacy of the Cross, and relied on God's forgiveness. He said this is like an athlete's training; the only way to do it is to step up and do it yourself.

> "Every athlete exercises self-control in all things. They do it to receive a perishable wreath, but we an imperishable [one]. ...[So] I pommel my body and subdue it" (1 Corinthians 9:25, 27).

> "I press on toward the goal for the prize of the upward call of God in Christ Jesus" (Philippians 3:13–14).

And he turns the same challenge on us:

"Present your bodies as a living sacrifice" (Romans 12:1).

What is left for us to do, in the story of salvation? Death has been vanquished, our sins are forgiven, the Father has accepted the self-offering of his Son. Yet we are still capable of sending ourselves to Hell, one self-indulgent decision at a time.

There is no room for complacency. We live on a spiritual battleground. Every day we must struggle against sin, against temptation, recognizing the tricks of the evil one and deflecting them. We must struggle against ourselves, reluctant though we be. We must get all the impurities out of our lump of coal, everything that will not burn.

You might be wondering, How did we get all the way over here? Isn't this a book about the Cross and atonement? How did we get to talking about personal prayer and spiritual disciplines? Can't we finish our theological discussion first?

But this *is* how it finishes. In Orthodoxy, the whole purpose of theology is theosis.

That's why it's so hard to explain the Orthodox view of salvation. It's not *only* the Cross; it's the whole story. It's vast and it's personal. It defies human comprehension, yet applies in the smallest junctures of our lives. In Orthodoxy all theology is practical, applied theology, and it is all mystical theology, guiding us to union with Christ. Our Western categories get jumbled. For salvation is much broader and more intimate than the Cross alone. It ultimately involves—everything, really.

21
PUTTING THEOLOGY TO WORK

There are many biblical puzzle-pieces to Christ's work of salvation, and they combine to produce a story that is both great and mysterious. Christ began our salvation by entering human nature and taking on our flesh, "being born in the likeness of men" (Philippians 2:7). Then he "bore our sins in his body on the tree" (1 Peter 2:24), and "humbled himself and became obedient unto death, even death on a cross" (Philippians 2:8).

- Christ **Rescued** the fallen human race by destroying "him who has the power of death, that is, the devil" (Hebrews 2:14).
- God **Forgives** us without payment, like the father of the Prodigal did. "When they could not pay, he forgave them" (Luke 7:41–42).
- And Christ sealed the "new covenant in [his] blood" (Luke 22:20), as a **Sacrifice** to the Father. Yet it was the Father who provided "the lamb for

the offering" (Genesis 22:8) and w"gave [us] his only Son" (John 3:16).

One unhappy consequence of the theological splintering of Western Christianity is that it became a shopper's market. As each variation insisted on its own particular interpretation of the Bible, the responsibility to discern the *right* interpretation gradually narrowed down, from a timeless community to a recent community to a family to an individual. Eventually, each individual was presumed competent to evaluate the theological and interpretive claims of these new traditions (there's an oxymoron). Thus individual opinion—perhaps not as competent as the individual supposed—gradually accumulated the full authority of a pope.

Meanwhile, churches discovered that they were now in competition with each other. Now they had to figure out how to attract and keep adherents, giving those potential adherents what they thought they wanted.

Strangely enough, and despite those churches' vast political, theological, and liturgical range, they somehow came to much the same conclusion. If you look at church signs, messaging, and ads, you'll find the emphasis is always on comfort and caring. The leading message to the public is "We care about you." But Jesus' leading message to his public was: "Repent" (Mark 1:14-15).

We may feel like comfort and caring is what we need most, though we are surely the most comfortable, if not pampered, generation in history. But Christ has better knowledge of the human heart. He gives us, instead, this challenge, and we come to him, without whining or excuses, ready to repent and begin to change. By his power we get stronger, maybe even strong enough to make hard changes. Christ himself comes to live within us. We become, if not in time, then at last in timelessness, the beloved person our Creator designed each of us to be.

Orthodoxy is not just a list of correct theological propositions (though I believe it *has* such propositions), not a mindfulness technique or a mystery cult. The Orthodox Church is surely not one of the great worldly powers. Orthodoxy is a Way—a way to be immersed in the life of Christ, he who died for us and rose again. It is a way to come into the presence of our loving Lord, and answer his call to at-one-ment.

ENDNOTES

2. BUT MY THEOLOGY IS BASED ON THE BIBLE!

1. You'd think the great Western theologians would read the New Testament in the original Greek. But St. Augustine disliked Greek as a child, and never learned it. Pope St. Gregory spent six years in Constantinople, but didn't acquire much of the language. St. Thomas Aquinas, supreme among Catholic theologians, is "generally supposed [to be] ignorant of Greek" says St. John Henry Newman, who translated Aquinas's *Catena*. Even though "his own words [in the *Catena*] seem to imply otherwise… he has in several cases quite missed the sense of the Greek."

3. RANSOMED, REDEEMED, DELIVERED, AND SAVED

1. Orthodox don't call this event "the harrowing of Hell" but "the Resurrection." Christ rose from the dead in Hades before he left his earthly tomb.
2. Why two different psalm numbers? Around 250-200 BC, Jewish scholars translated the Old Testament into koine Greek. This translation, the *Septuagint*, was the Bible of the early church. In it, the psalms are numbered differently.
3. *Epistle to the Magnesians* 9.
4. *Epistle to the Trallians* 9.
5. *Epistle to the Philippians* 1.
6. *Dialogue with Trypho* 72.
7. *Against Heresies* 5:31:1.
8. You really should experience this at least once in your life.

4. THE PRICE OF "SATISFACTION"

1. St. Anselm, *Cur Deus Homo?* 2.19
2. There's something oddly coincidental about the timing: Anselm promulgated his new theory just about the time East and West went their separate ways (the "Great Schism," AD 1054). Anselm's theory was little known in the East, and isn't compatible with Orthodox theology
3. As a contemporary worship song says, "Till on that Cross as Jesus died /

the wrath of God was satisfied."
4. John Calvin, *Institutes of the Christian Religion*, trans. Henry Beveridge, 2.16.10

5. MERITS AND OTHER MISCHIEF

1. Pope Clement VI (AD 1291–1352) established that the resources of the "treasury of merits" could be applied in the form of "indulgences," to lighten the temporal punishment for sin. See Catechism of the Catholic Church, §§1471, 1478–79, 1498.
2. St. Augustine, *On Forgiveness of Sins and Baptism* 1.19.
3. C. S. Lewis, *The Problem of Pain* (New York: Collier Books, 1962), 40.
4. I wonder if that song became so popular because people would actually *prefer* a God who kept his distance, and didn't take too active an interest in their daily lives.
5. That's why the best way to understand Orthodox theology is to look at the worship. The ancient services stay the same from century to century, nation to nation, and were able to teach the faith even to those who could not read. It's fine to read theologians, Church Fathers, or even books like this, but to really grasp the faith of the Orthodox community, go to Orthodox worship, and listen.
6. N.T. Wright, *The Day the Revolution Began* (New York: HarperOne, 2016), 26.

6. FORGIVENESS AND MERCY

1. Regarding that "as," someone called it "the most terrifying conjunction in the New Testament."
2. Forgiveness doesn't mean putting yourself at risk, for example, in an abusive relationship. Forgiveness addresses something in the past, but the present and future are a matter of *trust*. Forgiveness means that you set aside past deeds, deciding not to brood over them, or nurture fantasies of revenge. But you can continue to reserve trust until you see sufficient evidence that you will be safe.
3. James Bowman, *Honor: A History* (New York: Encounter, 2006), 59.
4. Scott Hahn, *Lord, Have Mercy* (New York: Doubleday, 2003).
5. St. Isaac of Syria, *The Ascetical Homilies* 51.251 (Boston, MA: Holy Transfiguration Monastery, 2011), 387.

7. SACRIFICES AND OFFERINGS

1. "A body you have prepared for me" is an eloquent foreshadowing of Christ's Incarnation, and that is how it reads in the Septuagint. But the Hebrew text is quite different: "Ears you have dug for me." English translations based on the Hebrew render this as something like, "You have given me an open ear."
2. N.T. Wright, *The Day the Revolution Began* (New York: HarperOne, 2016), 27.

8. WHO RECEIVES THE "RANSOM"?

1. Gustaf Aulén, *Christus Victor* (New York: Macmillan, 1969).
2. St. Gregory of Nyssa, *Great Catechism* 24. "In order to secure that the ransom in our behalf might be easily accepted by him who required it, the Deity was hidden under the veil of our nature, that so, as with ravenous fish, the hook of the Deity might be gulped down along with the bait of flesh."
3. St. Augustine, *Homilies* 261.1 (Benedictine numbering). "The devil jumped for joy when Christ died; and by the very death of Christ the devil was overcome: he took, as it were, the bait in the mousetrap. He rejoiced at the death, thinking himself death's commander. But that which caused his joy dangled the bait before him. The Lord's Cross was the devil's mousetrap: the bait which caught him was the death of the Lord."
4. St. Gregory Nazianzus, *Oration* 45.22.

UNTITLED

1. Leonid Ouspensky, *Theology of the Icon* (Crestwood, NY: St. Vladimir's Seminary Press, 1992), 1:78.
2. Matthew 27:35; Mark 15:24; Luke 23:33; John 19:18.

10. SIN AND RIGHTEOUSNESS

1. St. Augustine of Hippo, *On the Forgiveness of Sins* 21.
2. The theologian Abelard (AD 1079–1142) proposed that these children abide in a place (later called "Limbo") where they experience neither the sufferings of Hell nor the joys of Heaven. This view was taught in the Catholic Church for many centuries, but a document approved by Pope Benedict XVI suggests that there are "reasons for prayerful hope" that unbaptized babies are in Heaven.

3. St. Augustine, *On Forgiveness of Sins* 2.11.
4. *Catechism of the Catholic Church* (Collegeville, MN: Liturgical Press, 1994), §§1857–62.
5. Garrison Keillor, "Letter from Jim," *News from Lake Wobegon*, audio CD (High Bridge, 1990).

12. HADES, FIRE, AND THE EVIL ONE

1. In Greek it reads "the evil," using an adjective as a noun, as we might refer to "the rich and famous." Jesus uses this term again in the Parable of the Sower: "The evil one [the evil] comes and snatches away what was sown in his heart" (Matthew 13:19).
2. "Hades" is the koine Greek word the translators of the Septuagint used to represent the Hebrew *Sheol*. Both terms refer to a shadowy realm where the dead reside. When Adam and Eve were expelled from Paradise, the doors were shut to the human race (Genesis 3:23-24); but, by his Resurrection, Christ broke the grip of Hades and re-opened the way to Paradise.

    "Hell," on the other hand, represents *Gehenna,* the "Valley of the Son of Hinnom" outside Jerusalem. This was the accursed place where children were once burned to death as offerings to pagan gods. Jesus refers to *ge'enna* about a dozen times (e.g., Matthew 5:22, 5:29, 5:30, 10:28, 18:9, 23:15, 23:33), using it to mean the place where the evil one and those who follow him will suffer eternally.

13. THE PROBLEM OF EVIL

1. Luke 17:29
2. Matthew 5:22, 7:19, 13:42, 50, 18:8, 9, 25:41, 47-8
3. Matthew 8:12, 13:42, 13:50, 22:13, 24:51, 25:30, Luke 13:28.

14. MERCY AND REPENTANCE

1. St. Isaac of Syria, *The Ascetical Homilies* 28.141 (Boston: Holy Transfiguration Monastery, 2011), 266.

15. FREE WILL AND ASSURANCE OF SALVATION

1. St. John Cassian, *Conferences* 3.10–12.
2. Picture Mary doing this, helping the toddler Jesus learn to walk. He loves her so much.
3. St. Isaac of Syria, *The Ascetical Homilies of St. Isaac the Syrian* 39.192 (Boston, MA: Holy Transfiguration Monastery, 2011), 323.

16. HOW TO TURN INTO A GOAT

1. C. S. Lewis, *Mere Christianity* (New York: Touchstone, 1996), 176.

17. THE INCARNATION

1. St. Athanasius, *On the Incarnation* 2.9.
2. Though this line has been frequently attributed to Luther, and some of his writings come near it, no source has been found for the exact quote. Some Luther scholars feel that it is nevertheless in keeping with his soteriology. "Luther's 'Snow-Covered Dunghill': Myth?" Patheos.com, Dave Armstrong, April 7, 2016. http://www.patheos.com/blogs/davearmstrong/2016/04/luthers-snow-covered-dunghill-myth.html

18. EVERYWHERE PRESENT

1. "*Omnia recapitulans, recapitulatus est,*" that is, "Recapitulating everything, he is the recapitulation." Christ in himself sums up, completes, restores, fulfills all of Creation.
2. St. Irenaeus, Against Heresies 5.21.1. St. Irenaeus wrote in Greek, but only fragments remain, and his work is mostly available in Latin.

19. ENERGY AND SYNERGY

1. You may have encountered *energeia* before, in Aristotle, but the meaning is a bit different in Scripture.
2. "Power" is *dynamis*, whence we get "dynamite." St. Paul often pairs *energeia* with *dynamis*. Dynamis is the dynamite lying in a box; energeia is the explosion.
3. David Bradshaw, *Aristotle East and West: Metaphysics and the Division of Christendom* (Cambridge: Cambridge University Press, 2004), 264–65.

4. St. Macarius (Pseudo-Macarius), *Fifty Spiritual Homilies* 15.10.

20. THEOSIS

1. St. Cyril of Alexandria, *Commentary on St. Luke's Gospel*, Sermon 142.
2. St. John of Damascus, *On the Holy Images* 3.33.
3. St. Athanasius, *On the Incarnation* 54.3. St. Irenaeus of Lyons (ad 130–200) said much the same a century earlier, and repeatedly, though not as succinctly: *Against Heresies* 3.10.2; 3.18.7; 3.19.1; 3.33.4; 4.20.4; 5, preface.

www.ingramcontent.com/pod-product-compliance
Lightning Source LLC
Chambersburg PA
CBHW070612010526
44118CB00012B/1488